The Crown in Canada

THE CROWN IN CANADA

Frank MacKinnon

Glenbow-Alberta Institute
McClelland and Stewart West

Copyright © 1976 by Glenbow-Alberta Institute

Third printing, 1977

0-7712-1015-9 (casebound edition)

0-7712-1016-7 (paperbound edition)

McClelland and Stewart West
Calgary, Alberta

Printed and bound in Canada

ACKNOWLEDGEMENTS

I am grateful to many authorities and officials who have discussed this subject with me, especially those associated with the Crown. Work on this and other related projects was assisted by the University of Calgary, which gave me leave of absence; and by the Canada Council, which provided a leave fellowship and research grant. I appreciate very much the co-operation of the Department of External Affairs, and of the British Council, which arranged useful interviews abroad. I thank them all. Senator Eugene Forsey, pre-eminent authority on the Crown and invaluable Sherlock Holmes of Canadian political literature, read the manuscript; I am grateful for his observations and encouragement. Mr. David Scollard of McClelland and Stewart West edited the manuscript, and provided helpful suggestions. My wife's interest and co-operation were, as always, valuable contributions to my work.

CONTENTS

PREFACE

THE CROWN is a fundamental source of power in the Canadian constitution. It enables political institutions to operate the way they do, reinforces federalism, and supports democracy. It works so unobtrusively that many citizens are unaware it is at work at all—a fact which is an asset in its successful operation, although a hindrance to public appreciation of it.

The Crown is an elusive phenomenon and a practical institution of government. To some it seems like an old family ghost that has lingered for centuries doing little but making its presence felt. To others it is a remarkable political invention that makes much government action possible, fruitful, and tolerable. The Crown is still more than that. It is an institution at the summit of the state designed to limit the problems of wielding political power and to assist the interplay of human characteristics among officials and citizens, which are the real but unpredictable forces in public life.

The purpose of this book is to examine the Crown in Canadian government today, and the functions of its twelve representatives—the Queen, the Governor General, and the Lieutenant-Governors. The book is designed for general readers

9

and students; not as a theoretical, constitutional, or historical study, but as a practical assessment of a contemporary political institution.

A practical view of the Crown in Canada is incomplete without some comparison with alternatives. Like every institution, it has critics, some of whom claim "republican" sentiments and consider monarchy "undemocratic". We must consider this view seriously, and occasionally refer to alternatives, because it is a remarkable fact of world politics that democracy tends to work in constitutional monarchies, while it has died in numerous republics. Whether we like the fact or not, democracy is surviving with great difficulty, in an age when many governments around the world are failing in their service to their own people and their relations with other governments. Amid this confusion Canadians have a system that works, and they even enjoy their politics.

The reasons are not theoretical, but practical. It is the workability of the Crown that requires attention, not the theories of the "monarchist" and the "republican". These are unreliable categories anyway. A Canadian may say, for example, that he is a "monarchist" without appreciating the great difference between an absolute monarchy and a constitutional one, or understanding that the reasons for having a monarch are more practical than sentimental. Another Canadian may claim he is a "republican" without admitting that many republics are absolute monarchies under another name, and that under the Crown his cabinet, parliament, and fellow citizens have more political power than their counterparts in most republics.

Some observers, particularly in Quebec, have recently criticized the Crown and the Queen in relation to alleged British domination, and the Governor General and Lieutenant-Governor as symbols of the "federal presence". We shall examine these criticisms, and assess the Crown and its representatives in relation to national unity and diversity and to the facts of political life in Quebec and the other provinces.

There is an inevitable problem in gathering material on this subject. Individuals directly concerned with the Crown's powers are generous in describing what goes on, and I have interviewed many of them. But they do not want details associated publicly with contemporary people and events. This is the only suitable approach in relation to the Crown. No governor should tell for publication his relations with a premier. No premier will announce what help a governor gave him. No officials can publish the ways in which the non-partisan powers and functions of the Crown were used to settle difficult problems or expedite delicate matters. Almost all such incidents take place, where they should take place in matters concerning the Crown in a democracy, behind the scenes, quietly, confidentially, and in an atmosphere of trust.

Like an iceberg, the Crown displays only its tip. The rest of it concerns realities of politics and human nature, which in most institutions tend to be hidden from the general view, or suspected but not admitted in the conventional wisdom.

I have therefore organized the material into two kinds of chapters. The first three deal with major obstacles to an understanding of the Crown. We too often consider what the Crown does without examining first *why* it exists to do it. And we frequently emphasize features of the Crown without considering the characteristics of governments and citizens which gave rise to them. After discussing these matters, we will proceed in Chapter Four to examine the work of the Queen, Governor General, and Lieutenant-Governors. I hope Chapters Four to Nine will show what these officials do in Canada's governments, and provide illustrations for the earlier discussions of the Crown's place in the democracy of which it is a vital part.

F.M.
The University of Calgary
1975

ONE

THE POLITICAL SETTING

"GOD SAVE THE QUEEN" really means "God help us to govern ourselves". We are not very good at it sometimes. One reason is the uncertainty of both political leadership and the response to it of the citizenry. The Crown exists to help relieve this difficulty. The anthem goes on, in a later, rarely heard verse, to condemn our enemies: "Confound their politics, frustrate their knavish tricks." The Crown is designed to assist our own politics and compensate for our own tricks.

Man needs this compensation. He is difficult to lead because he is inclined to stampede easily or to refuse to budge. To direct his public affairs and get him to participate effectively in them takes a degree of skill possessed by few people. Who these people are, how they are to be selected, what powers should be given them, how they should exercise these powers, and how they are to be removed from office have been argued since men combined in groups. Yet, after centuries of experience, it is extraordinary how ambivalent man still is to leadership, and how unpredictable is leadership itself. It is not surprising, therefore, that man invents many ideologies and systems in attempting to determine satisfactorily the duties of leaders and citizens. Even a quick glance at every continent indicates he is not doing very well. But he continues to invent.

One invention, the Crown, stands out among man's numerous political institutions. Associated with government for centuries, it has taken many forms with varying success and failure. Until modern times the powers of the Crown were entrusted to an "absolute monarch". He actually ruled on his own initiative; although he had advisers, he, not they, took responsibility for the policy and action. Following much political experience, the old powers of absolute monarchy have largely been suspended in most kingdoms. A sovereign now is usually a "constitutional monarch". He does not rule personally, but just "reigns"; he acts on the advice of ministers to whom responsibility has been delegated by the people. Constitutional monarchy developed slowly, and the idea of reigning but not ruling took a long time to understand. They are modern innovations designed to meet problems of leadership that have developed in all systems of government. With this primary purpose, and still retaining many old traditions, powers, and decorative functions that have proved useful, the Crown operates in mysterious and practical ways in, of all places, the modern democratic state.

At this point it is essential to define the "Crown" and the "democratic state". Even though these definitions may appear legalistic, they help to reveal certain unwarranted assumptions and unsuspected facts, of which there are obviously many in politics. The term "Crown" is used in every monarchy; and almost all states call themselves "democratic". But the Crown in Canada is not the same as the Crown in Iran. A Canadian's idea of democracy is different from that of a Bulgarian. Unfortunately for the Crown, men confuse it with the concept of the sovereign. Unfortunately for democracy, that term has become so fashionable that men confuse it with many things, including its opposites. Canadians speak of democracy in a system of responsible government which involves a partnership of Crown and parliament. This point is essential. It is easy to talk grandly of "government of the people, for the people, by the people"– everybody does it, including dictators. But democracy involves much more than that, as Canadians know who observe undemocratic methods of governing being carried out in its name in so-called democracies elsewhere. Even in countries closely associated with Canada, like France and the United States, there are institutions and processes which Canadians would not call "democratic", such as the

14

French president's relations with his parliament, or the U.S. president's power to conduct war.

What, then, is the Crown, and how does it function as an institution of democratic government in Canada?

The Crown is the supreme executive power of the state, above the structure of government in the state, and designed as a point in the constitution from which other powers are created, measured, and controlled. It is not the sovereign. It is an executive power–that is, a power concerned with safeguarding the laws and implementing their provisions, as well as devising policy and supervising its execution. There are other powers: legislative (making laws), judicial (interpreting laws), and administrative (carrying out detailed procedures provided by laws). These powers are associated with executive power in many ways to provide the leadership without which no state can operate.

The turbulent history of executive power, and the problems associated with it in many countries today, indicate that its effectiveness depends greatly on who possesses it. Despite intricate ideological and constitutional arrangements, possessors of power have made many mistakes, and sometimes even destroyed their power and ruined their state through stupidity. Consequently an arrangement gradually evolved through trial and error that separated the *possession* of power from the *wielding* of power. That is, one institution would possess the power without wielding it, and another would wield the power without possessing it. This is the arrangement we now have in Canada. Even though we may associate executive power with certain officials, we do not in law or in fact make it the personal possession of any of them. We put it outside the governmental structure, not in someone's hands, but in an abstraction, and we call that abstraction the Crown. Once we did give the power to a person, the sovereign. But that did not always work satisfactorily, because sovereigns, like politicians, are human and fallible. We therefore gradually, and over many decades, separated the sovereign from the Crown by making him just a personification of the Crown and the custodian of its powers. As a custodian, a much-different official from a possessor of powers, the sovereign holds the powers on behalf of the people, and he or she is the personal symbol of authority which man finds necessary to have in every system. But the sovereign may not normally wield these powers personally. While his position was changing in this way, the role of his senior minister, or prime minister, evolved from a principal adviser into a head of government. The sovereign remained head of state, but the prime minister assumed the leadership of the state's administration and the responsibility for its decisions and actions. The sovereign must therefore act on the advice of his prime minister.

Why do we need the two? As we shall note in more detail later, citizens may wish to elect, support, criticize, and remove the prime minister at their will. However, it has proved difficult, and in many states impossible, for citizens to control him if he is also the head of state. So we ask the sovereign to look after the pomp which is inevitable in government and be a custodian of the powers, while we instruct the prime minister to advise on the use of the powers (as we may determine or ask our elected representatives to determine), but not to covet any of the power himself. Neither he nor the cabinet are even mentioned in Canada's basic constitutional document, the British North America Act, which refers only to the Queen in connection with executive power! This seemingly extraordinary omission is logical in view of experience with over-powerful prime ministers. On behalf of parliament and the people it reveals them as trustees to whom much responsibility can be entrusted, but also readily taken away. And it puts them clearly on the defensive at election time in an era when several heads of government elsewhere possess so much power they are able to control elections or abolish them altogether.

The Crown is therefore a means of meeting a difficulty, so evident in history and contemporary politics throughout the world, of preventing officials at the summit of government from becoming too powerful, irresponsible, and perhaps immovable.

Does this mean that there is no single person in the entire structure of government who actually possesses and wields at his own discretion the executive powers of the state? It means exactly this.

What about the people? Democratic theory assumes that all political power ultimately rests with the people. It does; but there are limitations to this great principle. The people are not effectively organized to wield the political powers of their state except through their governments. Public opinions are conflicting and difficult to assess. Most important of all, there are groups within the people who justify their ideas and actions on their conviction that they speak for the people as a whole and know what is good for them. They may be right. But they may presume too much and be wrong; for them to snatch power may be disas-

16

trous. We therefore protect the power of the people by putting it in the Crown, thereby enabling the people to invoke it as they wish, but actually assign it only to those among them who have their confidence.

If this arrangement seems intangible, it is not unique. The Crown in government resembles the soul of man in philosophy, and the algebraic x in mathematics—the one powerful and the other useful. It also invites even more practical comparisons. People often set up "trusts" for the performance of certain acts, and appoint "trustees" to wield necessary authority. Were a man and his wife to die, for example, they would not be found to have left their money directly to their young children for them to handle; indeed the laws would not permit it if they did. Nor would they have given the money to someone to spend for the children. Their estate is placed in trust. The trustees control it, but do not possess it; the children possess it, but do not control it. Yet another familiar analogy may be employed. Engineers, surveyors, builders, and construction workers use a benchmark, or fixed location *separate* from a structure for surveys and observations so that distances, directions, and levels may be ascertained, in order that the structure may be accurately built and precisely related to other structures.

For citizens who go beyond the mind of man to his soul for the meaning of life, or use "let x equal. . ." to solve complicated problems, who protect their families and money by means of trusts, and measure their structures from points detached from those structures, it is not surprising that in constitutional monarchies they follow a similar practice in protecting themselves from misuse of the political powers of their state.

If we say the Crown operates effectively in a democracy, what do we mean by a democracy? Definitions are legion in the world, indeed within any one state, including Canada. The word is in danger of becoming a meaningless slogan because of the wrong use of it, and because people are more inclined to invoke it than to live up to it. We must therefore define the term in a discussion of this kind.

Democracy involves a distinction between the *state*, or the organized political association of people with a recognized government; and the *community*, or the total group of citizens within the bounds of the state organized for all activities of life, including political ones. The people thus constitute *both* a state and a community. This distinction is necessary because people's lives in-

17

clude more than political indentities and activities. Democracy also involves the recognition that the law is above governments and the latter are subject to the law. There are fundamental constitutional provisions and rights which the government may not abolish and the people must observe. The free play of conflicting opinions must be brought to bear in constitutional ways on the selection of government and on the judgment of its actions, as well as on the groups and individuals of which the community is composed. If government or any community action is to be of, for, and by the people these requirements are essential. This concept of democracy is the one we will use in this book.[1]

Having a Crown in a democracy may seem a contradiction. It would be if "Crown" implied absolute monarchy, and if democracy merely meant government of, for, and by the people. Dignified and wishful rhetoric notwithstanding, absolutism has not worked in the long run, people are rarely co-ordinated in their opinions and actions, and evil leadership can do evil things to popular wishes. Both absolutism and majority rule have often been tragically wrong. But because they inevitably turn up in some form in any system of government, we gradually recognized both, and, over a long period of time, combined them, altered them, and surrounded them with a network of limitations in order to encourage their best attributes and prevent their worst liabilities.

The political purist may support either absolutism or majority rule in some form, and consider any limit on them to be unrealistic or irrelevant. But he must always ask what he would want were he opposed to the absolute authority; or if he belonged to a minority persecuted by a tyrannical majority, or a majority persecuted by a tyrannical minority. This question played a major part in developing the Crown in democracy. That it has not yet been answered at all in many republics is evident from the plaintiveness of those who ask it and from the upheavals that accompany its neglect.

We should also define the term "republic" because it is often used wrongly as the opposite of "monarchy", and therefore assigned to some states which are neither republican nor democratic. A republic, says the Oxford Dictionary, is "a state in which the government is carried on nominally and usually in fact also by the people or through its elected representatives." A constitutional monarchy can thus be a republic too, because its government is actually carried on, not by the sovereign, but by and

18

through the people's representatives in the name of the people. On the other hand, to consider a state a republic simply because it has no sovereign, or to think it democratic because it operates in the name of the people, are both wrong and naive. Greece, for example, did not, by our definition, become a republic when King Constantine was replaced by President Papadopoulos in 1973; the latter was not elected. Military regimes are not republics. And countries where elections give the people no real choice are not republics either. Even if the wording of the definition were arguable, it is the spirit and actual fact that determine the character of governments. On both these counts too, a constitutional monarchy can be a republic, and a republic in name can be an absolute monarchy in fact. In using the term "republic" in this book and elsewhere, we should therefore appreciate how unreliable it is.

It must be noted, for example, that there are many kinds of "republics", and variations within each kind. Some carefully protect the distinctions between powers of parliaments and powers of governments; others do not. Some are controlled by the military. Civil rights are secure in some, ignored in others. Elections are effective in some, farcical in others. In some "republics" the president is both head of state and head of government; in others he is just head of state. In some his powers, definable in law, are rarely used. In others they are unlimited in practice. Indeed several presidents in this last category outdo absolute monarchs of by-gone days in wielding personal power.

This last point is vital today. Citizens who make comparisons between constitutional monarchies and republics must clearly understand that republicanism is practised in constitutional monarchy, while absolute monarchy flourishes in many so-called republics. People tend to think only of the styles and titles of monarchy, and neglect the fact that monarchal ways of governing, which are powerful characteristics of a system, may continue or arise without them. Britain, the Benelux countries, Scandinavia, and many Commonwealth countries retained and altered their monarchies to suit the rise of democratic government by removing monarchal ways of governing, but also retained the styles and titles of monarchy for reasons which will be discussed later. Considering the definition of democracy suggested above, they are now democracies in fact. Meanwhile other countries shook off the forms of monarchy in the alleged interest of democratic aspirations, national pride, people's government, and other concepts.

19

But most of them did not dispose of or alter monarchal ways of governing. This form of governing thereupon continued to be absolute with many presidents who succeeded kings, and in some political parties that embraced with delight monarchy's oldest autocratic powers.

Thus we have a paradox. Many heads of state who are in effect absolute monarchs are now called presidents of republics. And many political parties, especially the communist party and several others in one-party states, show all the arrogance and exclusiveness of the more authoritarian and imperialistic of ancient royal courts. The comparison even applies in a much more modest way to the United States and France where, despite elections and democratic theory, the presidents are closer to the monarchism of George III and Louis XIV than are Queen Elizabeth II, her representatives, and her prime ministers, either singly as officials or together as an executive. It is significant that Professor Arthur M. Schlesinger Jr. called his recent book "The Imperial Presidency", and Le Monde speaks of the French head of state as a "monarque-président". "I never felt so 'royal'," said L.B. Pearson, "as in the French Republic."[2]

Theorists, concentrating on form based on ideologies, tend to ignore these facts. Indeed they are often sympathetic to what is absolute monarchy in republics while declaring constitutional monarchy as being against their principles! A church leader illustrated the matter when criticized by a lady for believing in polygamy. "But," he protested, "I don't practice polygamy; I have only one wife." "I don't care," she persisted, "it is the principle of the thing." "In that case," came the reply, "I would rather be a polygamist who monogs than a monogamist who polygs." Democracy is safer under a monarch who "repubs" than a republican who "monarchs".

There is one more definition basic to these discussions. It is fundamental in any democratic system. Like the others, the term "responsible government" has been much used and abused. The concept is based on two facts: those who exercise power do it better when they and their work are subjected to the opinions of others; and those who propose things are more sensible in their demands if they have some involvement in carrying them out. Anyone can govern with a completely free hand, but he can be wrong. Anyone can put forward attractive ideas, but they can be impractical. We therefore include in our system mechanisms by which those who govern must have their work appraised, and those whose business is done must have their opinions assessed.

These mechanisms have proved difficult to guarantee and make work when political power is placed in the possession of a person, group, or office. Leaders sometimes think they know what is good for everyone without adequate consultation and advice. They may grab power and not account for it, or destroy other leaders and silence critics if they have the chance. Or they may be weak, and neglect the responsibilities of power. We therefore place the power of the state with the Crown, and make special arrangements by which those who would use it must give evidence of their intentions and accounts of their jurisdictions. After all the turbulence in the history of power wielding, it is remarkable to be able to say, even to the head of government and the smallest minority group: "There is the power of the state; if you want to use some of it, by all means ask; we will never *give* it to you, although we may make you a temporary trustee of it; but first we must know your intentions and later we will hold you accountable."

These definitions have obvious limitations and are open to interpretation. When citizens examine the constitutional arrangements of their state they find that it is impossible to define exactly the principles and practices they desire. There are too many variables. The personalities and abilities of prime ministers, for example, cause variety in administrative practice and executive leadership, no matter what rules are set down. Some officials are able, some are mediocre, some are inept, and these attributes affect the operation of political institutions, including the cabinet. It is difficult to anticipate how a government should act in crisis. The size of a majority in parliament will determine controls on a government. The desires of citizens change with political fashions and with good times and bad. Even formal principles are inadequate expressions of fact; what is democratic to one person may not be to another; what is responsible government to one party may be arrogant management to its opponents.

Most constitutions that work well therefore include both a written part in the form of documents which set down firm rules, and an unwritten part consisting of many other rules, precedents, practices, and customs which are sufficiently understood to be followed, and flexible enough to meet variations in personalities and situations. Thus the Canadian constitution is not just the British North America Act and other statutes, but also a large accumulation of less tangible, but nevertheless effective, observances which have proved useful over a long period of time, under a wide variety of leaders, and with continually changing public opinion. The Crown in public life protects many of the written specifications, and permits and sponsors the operation of numerous effective observances.

One example illustrates all our definitions–that of Her Majesty's Loyal Opposition. The opposition is not mentioned in the written part of the constitution; indeed, how could one accurately describe it and its role in a formal document? The phrase seems silly in relation to the exalted expectations of government. Why should there be a "loyal" opposition at all? Some countries call people in this category traitors. We call them loyal so no-one will think of them as traitors. But is it possible to be loyal when opposing a government? Many leaders used and still use the block, the noose, the guillotine, or the firing squad to answer that question. We therefore make it clear that loyalty to the state and loyalty to the government are different things which are often opposed. We say that the opposition is not the government's to be treated as the government may wish, but a group entitled "Her Majesty's" and "loyal" to indicate that it has a recognized status which the government cannot assault, that its functions of opposing are constitutional and respectable, and that it is in the interest of the state that the government should be opposed. Thus legitimate status for the opposition comes from outside the entire structure of government, so much so that one can even criticize Her Majesty and get away with it, a privilege not permitted by many republican heads of state.*

Why not, one may ask, call it the "people's opposition"? It does serve the people in practice; but the people's auspices of official oppositions have proved most unreliable in numerous countries. Indeed many "people's republics" are actually dictatorships in which the people have little power or freedom and there is no opposition. Groups within the people have a habit of undermining, perhaps even persecuting, oppositions in the name

---

*The effectiveness of Mr. Willie Hamilton's arguments in *My Queen and I* (London, Quartet, 1974) are weakened or rendered untenable when one considers how few republics there are in which he could be critical of the head of state and be permitted to retain a seat in parliament, perhaps even his life. His freedom to criticize is one of the main reasons for having the Crown. And his criticisms are generally more applicable to many republics.

of all the people, especially when charismatic government leaders or authoritarian ideologies encourage them to do so. In fact numerous contemporary oppositions are struggling to maintain their existence, let alone their ability to oppose governments, and many are ignored or have disappeared. And it is often the people who encourage this decline or destruction, either directly or through indifference, usually to repent their loss later. Meanwhile Canadian politicians who spent long, frustrating years trying to make dents in the armour of powerful men like Premiers Smallwood, Duplessis, and W.A.C. Bennett, were able to work away respectably despite indifferent support from the public and the overwhelming power of the government, ultimately to overthrow the government without the slightest taint of disloyalty or even a suggestion of constitutional damage or civil war. It is remarkable how uncommon this arrangement is in the world.

We have noted the partnership of Crown and parliament in Canadian government as a feature of our democracy. It is provided by statute that the Parliament of Canada consists of "the Queen, an Upper House styled the Senate and the House of Commons".[3] This partnership provides further examples of the definitions of the Crown, democracy, and responsible government. Its purpose is to strengthen parliament.

Canadians have so many stable legislatures they are inclined to take parliamentary government for granted. Yet it cannot safely be taken for granted. Its long, slow evolution over many centuries indicates how hard it was to get a parliament established. And the impotence or disappearance of parliaments in many countries emphasizes the fact that, however elegantly the principles of parliament may be extolled, their actual operation, indeed their very existence, is worthy of respect. Even in countries with long and honourable parliamentary traditions, it is easy to criticize parliamentary practice and consider parliaments weak in the face of encroaching technology and bureaucracy.

All levels of government from monarch to citizen have assaulted parliaments at one time or another. But the most frequent offender is the executive, or government of the day, sometimes backed by the people. A party may burn a parliament, as the Nazis did the Reichstag. Administrations, especially when backed by huge majorities and popular acclaim, will encourage the rubber stamp theory in even the most democratically organized legislatures. It is a complaint of parliaments, even in the Commonwealth, that prime ministers encourage a "presidential system" by ignoring parliament. And in republics which have a president-parliament relationship, such as France, it has been the complaint even of ministers, that a de Gaulle will by-pass both parliament and government if an opportunity presents itself.

The executive may not, however, be entirely at fault. Inherent limitations of democracy may also threaten parliamentary government. Representatives of the people do come together to discuss the people's business and the government's management, and to propose and give approval to the legislation. And the government does hold office only so long as it has the support of parliament. But two limitations determine the effectiveness of these great principles. One is the fact that politicians, like everyone else, tend to talk and argue more readily than they act, and all kinds of arrangements must be made to get them to make up their minds, and to translate the results of debate into action. That we admit this is evident in a fat book of parliamentary rules and forms and in the controls of parliament's agenda. The other limitation is often suspected and talked about privately, but it is rarely admitted out loud. Some members are competent legislators and representatives of the people. Some are incompetent. Some are temperamental nuisances whom parliament could well do without. This limitation is common among deliberative bodies, and it is not realistic to think that membership in a parliament automatically denotes wisdom and competence, or even adequate representation of the people. Indeed, personal deficiencies of members have been among the factors in the by-passing and downfall of parliaments.

For these reasons, the Canadian constitution, like others of the same type, features a distinction between the institution of parliament itself and the existing collection of its members, as well as a dependence of parliament and the executive on each other. That is why so many traditions are associated with parliament, why so many strange but workable forms and practices are followed in it. Bowing to the Speaker, calling a man the honourable member instead of Mr. Smith, providing a smoking room where much business really takes place, are not frills, but vital psychological concessions to human nature. Parliamentary privilege may seem an anachronism sometimes, but the way members have behaved toward one another and other people have behaved toward them makes it a practical necessity. It is frighteningly easy for a parliament to forget itself, its responsibilities, even the very reason for its existence, when facing the exigencies of a temporary situation or the interest of an impatient group. It is also easy for a people to forget during some passing excitements or unspectacular interludes why they have a parliament and what it means as a cornerstone of their democracy. If it dies, it is too late to revive it; the long process of building one must usually be undertaken again.

Making the sovereign a part of parliament is one of the devices which emphasize the parliament in relation to both the government of the day and the temporary collection of its members, and highlight the interest of both the state and the people. "The Monarchy as it exists now," wrote the great labour leader and parliamentarian Herbert Morrison, "facilitates the processes of parliamentary democracy and functions as an upholder of freedom and representative government."[4] Prime Minister Robert Menzies of Australia made a similar observation. "The Queen is seen in all the countries within her allegiance as the fountain of honour, the protector of the law, the centre of a Parliamentary system in which she makes and proclaims statutes 'by and with the advice and consent' of Parliament. . .the Crown remains the centre of our democracy; a fixed point in the whirl of circumstance."[5] To some such a fixed point may seem mythical. But its reality stands out when the whirl of circumstance becomes erratic or violent. A biographer of U.S. presidents put the matter clearly, and illustrated the sovereign's advantage over the president. "The true crime of Richard Nixon," wrote Theodore H. White, "was simple; he destroyed the myth that binds America together. . .that somewhere in American life there is at least one man who stands for law, the president."[6]

The law receives with royal assent the sanction, not just of a government, but of the state. "My government", a phrase used by the sovereign and her representatives on formal occasions, implies that the government is not the prime minister's. He is the Crown's minister, and a temporary chairman of the cabinet who has limited formal powers, a situation many other heads of government are not forced to recognize.* While parliament is summoned and dissolved by the sovereign or her representative on

---

*Citizens who identify governments only by the name of the prime minister, a convenient practice most follow in referring, for example, to the "Bennett government" or the "Pearson government", may appreciate the significance of the distinction described when they serve on committees of groups like the board of trade or the faculty of a university, and

the advice of the prime minister, he and everyone else know it is not his to tamper with. What is discussed in parliament is the Crown's business, not the government's, a distinction based on much sad experience. The Commons still introduces a *pro forma* bill, without intending to pass it, at the beginning of each session, before discussing the Speech from the Throne which is written by the government, in order to remind the government and the representative of the Crown of a constitutional principle which is often ignored elsewhere–that the Crown's business is the people's business. And in debate the free speech of members is bolstered by the fact that no-one in the House has any power to invoke sanctions against them. The opposition enjoys the status already described. As for that powerful element which so often interferes with parliaments in republics, the military, it has no role in government at all. It takes its oath to the Crown; neither government nor opposition can command its interventions in governing; it can dictate neither the composition nor the decisions of parliament.

It may be said that all this is form, but not fact. It is form, and it *is* fact. But we do not readily see the fact, except when crisis and comparisons with other governments highlight it. When, for example, students of political science consider that ponderous and seemingly archaic relic, the royal prerogative of the dissolution of parliament, they may think it an academic subject. And it takes some exercise in probabilities for them to consider democratic a royal power to dismiss ministers which sovereigns and their representatives do not want to use. But during the months of the Newfoundland crisis of 1971-72, for instance, when the Smallwood government lost its majority in the legislature and appeared loath to resign, these powers were sympathetically considered and enthusiastically advocated, especially when the then leader of the opposition and later premier, Frank Moores, publicly asked that the dismissal power be used by the Lieutenant-Governor.* As for comparisons with other countries, every situation in the preceding paragraph may be contrasted with practices in republics which Canadians would not tolerate in their own legislatures. Indeed, many presidents, acting like absolute

---

hear some chairman refer to "my committee". "Who does he think he is?" is the usual reaction; and it is one of which prime ministers need occasional reminders.

Globe & Mail, Dec. 2, 1971

monarchs because there is no Crown to prevent them from doing so, are able to weaken or destroy legislatures. But "surely such things could never happen here": those were famous last words in many countries where parliamentary government died.

Queen Elizabeth II best stated what does happen in the Canadian system. "The role of a constitutional monarch," she said in Quebec in 1964, "is to personify the democratic state, to sanction legitimate authority, to assure the legality of its measures, and to guarantee the execution of the popular will. In accomplishing this task, it protects the people against disorder."[7]

Canada inherited this constitutional arrangement from Britain when she was just a group of undeveloped colonies with no political experience, and then proceeded to make it her own. Although based at first on powers of colonial governors transmitted by formal documents, the structure expanded, developed, and became autonomous as the colonies and later Canada grew into economically and politically adept societies. The development was gradual; it had to be in a huge, under-populated land with untapped resources and little affluence. This fact is often misunderstood. Canada did not achieve independence in a brave struggle against abject colonialism or domineering imperialism; she attained it when she matured and was able to handle it and pay for it herself. Thus the constitution had time to take hold. The result was a rare situation among the nations of the world–two centuries of workable government and a peaceful political life for citizens. Indeed Canada's Crown-parliament-people relationship is one of the most modern, advanced forms of democracy in the world. What! one might exclaim, modern? Yes, modern. Many countries are now at the political stage Canada passed long ago during struggles for representative and responsible government. For example, the reforms promised in Spain in February, 1974 by President* Carlos Arias Navarro read like the concessions granted by colonial governors in the 1830's and 1840's. So do those suggested a month later by Emperor Haile Selassie of Ethiopia. The problems of government in almost all the countries of South America and Africa and in many governments in Europe and Asia are often reminiscent of the criticisms of Baldwin, Lafontaine, Mackenzie, Howe, and other reformers in Canada's colonial days.

Canada had the advantage of receiving a pre-tested and still

*In other states he would be called "Premier".

developing political system. Britain had been experimenting with it for many centuries, trying out this tactic, discarding that. Indeed, the constitution developed by itself as experience with all kinds of public officials and events dictated. It was not built like a house; it grew like a tree. It evolved with King John's experiences, the lessons of Cromwell's time, the wisdom of some monarchs and ministers and the stupidities of others, the special compensations for the strengths and weaknesses of executive committees which had to be introduced into cabinets, and the long difficult task of assembling several hundred individuals representing countless viewpoints into a big chamber so they could do properly the business of the state. And all this is not yet finished. Neither human nature nor the characteristics of government have changed fundamentally in all that time, and each constitutional development is therefore of practical relevance to contemporary public life.

Canada also had the advantage of developing her constitution in comparative isolation. She had only one near neighbour, in contrast to other countries that had several, often hostile, neighbours, that were occasionally overrun, and that were bombarded with alien ideologies and practices that did not work well on their soil. Canada's one neighbour, the United States, contributed federalism to our constitutional discussions more than a century ago, and we adopted the idea. But the Americans had been developing federalism during the century prior to that, and, conveniently for Canada, had a civil war at the time of our discussions, which warned us to be cautious in adopting that system and blending it with the Crown-parliament tradition. Thus the Canadian constitution evolved while incorporating centuries of experience from across the seas and up-to-date results of the new system next door—in total an enormous political heritage—without interference by snooping, meddling neighbours. At Confederation this heritage was assembled and its basic principles were given expression through the British North America Act which was the work of the Canadian statesmen who planned and drafted it without interference from outside. From then on the constitution continued to grow with the new nation, and became a uniquely Canadian institution. It settled into the Canadian environment in Canadian ways, in the light of Canadian characteristics and problems; and, most important of all, it adjusted itself to accommodate the varied abilities and temperaments of Canadian leaders.

Such comparatively smooth adjustment is not without penalty. There was no major war or revolution to stimulate intense nationalism, no repulsed enemy to provide the heady intoxications of victory, no spectacular heroes to raise the excitements of martyrdom and great causes. These are powerful stimuli to budding nationhood and growing community spirit. Despite the unreliability they have so often demonstrated elsewhere, the lack of these sensations has made Canadian constitutional development seem so dull that historians have valiantly tried to dress up every minor skirmish as a major event, and few citizens appreciate the virtues of their constitution. Macdonald and Cartier would probably have insisted that this situation was the best and most peaceful in which to launch a new nation.

The beneficial result was emphasized a century later by Governor General Léger. "I have great admiration for the Canadian political system and its institutions," he declared. "Down through the centuries, Canadians have evolved a system under the Crown which is well adapted to our country and to our character. This political system is of great value. It has enabled us to develop as a free people and a united people, despite our vast territory and cultural diversity."[8]

These inheritances and adaptations have given Canadians a constitution which is stronger than they suspect, and a political life which is more peaceful than they appreciate. Certainly there are problems, but, by world standards, Canadians do not know what political trouble is. Why? One of the lessons of history is that constitutions do not serve people, as distinct from governments, when they are fashioned from "logical" systems, without allowances for the fact that men do not always act logically; or when they are designed on the basis of attractive political "blueprints", without examination of the cultural and economic foundations on which the governmental structure rests; or when they are based on "pure" ideologies which, inevitably becoming impure in encounters with reality, lead to the destruction of the principles on which they were founded. Illustrations are legion in the twentieth century. The problem lies in the nature of "logic", "blueprints", and "purity". They do not stand up by themselves. Like pure steel, they shine and are strong. But, without counterparts of alloy, they are brittle, and even a small, sharp tap may crack or shatter them. There is nothing logical or pure about the Canadian constitution, and it looks like a complicated blueprint. It has much political alloy to compensate for human practices inserted in vulnerable places. By any comparison, it works.

The Fathers of Confederation examined carefully the Crown and decided that it would continue to work in Canada. "I believe," declared Sir John A. Macdonald on the monarchal principle, "that it is of the utmost importance to have that principle recognized, so that we shall have a Sovereign who is placed above the region of party–to whom all parties look up–who is not elevated by the action of one party nor depressed by the action of another, who is the common head and sovereign of all."[9] "In this country," said Sir George E. Cartier, "we should have a distinct form of government, the characteristic of which would be to possess the monarchical element."[10] Respecting French-speaking Canadians, he asserted: "If they had their institutions, their language and their religion intact to-day, it was precisely because of their adherence to the British Crown."* This approach was practical in view of the political troubles of the day in many republics and the civil war in the United States. "The Fathers of the Confederation," writes Professor Creighton, "had good reason for believing that constitutional monarchy on the British model was the best government for free men that had yet been devised."[11]

The Fathers would likely find the same kind of reasons for the same belief were they alive to-day. The Crown's success in Canada has been obvious by any comparison. It has helped government to function for two hundred years in two such different units as Ontario, which is bigger and more populous than many countries, and Prince Edward Island, that is smaller than many counties and has fewer people than many cities. It strengthened

---

*The subject of Quebec in the system will be discussed in the final chapter of this book. Cartier's comment is a reminder of several facts. France paid only limited attention to Quebec just prior to the war of 1756-63 and did not lament its loss. And Britain was not sure whether she was to be congratulated or sympathized with on the acquisition of any of the undeveloped and expensive colonies of the north. Although victory in war determined the change, Britain did a generous, if convenient, thing for those days–she continued Quebec's institutions and guaranteed her language and religion. Many other states have enforced alien arrangements rigorously in similar circumstances, and even persecuted those who sought to follow their old ways. Those who would deny Cartier's assertion should state what else should have been done in 1763 in relation to the facts of the time, and what viable alternatives, including absorption into the United States, should have been followed in the

the union of 1867 because it was the only symbol the provinces had in common. Because of its kind of power the federal government can accommodate such different prime ministers as John Diefenbaker, L.B. Pearson, and Pierre Trudeau in the same decade without major adjustments. The cabinet has had two spectacular mutinies (in the governments of Mackenzie Bowell and John Diefenbaker) without a banishment, assassination, or rearrangement of apparatus when the government fell. Governments have been defeated; none has been deposed. Two founding peoples have quarrelled, as similar groups do regularly elsewhere, but they have not fought for over two centuries. There are eleven governments, not one. Only two of the partners, Quebec and Ontario, entered the union willingly; the rest raised commotions, had to be enticed, and joined with misgiving. As for the citizens, they sing "We stand on guard" no less than five times in their one-verse national anthem, and yet they have had to do less standing on guard than any people on earth. This extraordinary situation is exceptional in contemporary government, and the Crown as a constitutional umbrella and an emotional symbol helps to sustain it. Some Canadians know all this; some are unaware of it and chase ideological aurora; many suspect it and wonder how it is done.

---

next century. Speaking in Halifax on September 10, 1864, George Etienne Cartier said of Quebec:–"I am living in a Province in which the inhabitants are monarchical by religion, by habit and by the remembrance of past history. Our great desire and our great object in making efforts to obtain the federation of the Provinces is not to weaken monarchical institutions, but on the contrary to increase their influence." Edward Whelan, *Confederation of the Provinces*, Charlottetown, G.T. Hazard, 1865, p. 26.

TWO

THE HUMAN SETTING

THE CROWN must be regarded with human sensitivity as well as constitutional logic. It is easy but futile to devise institutions without making allowances for the characteristics of people. Just how easy is evident in the failure of numerous constitutions in our time, most of which were splendid in theory, but unworkable. The Crown illustrates the impact of human nature on democratic government, and how it must be compensated for in all political institutions.

This impact may be considered as either psychological or organizational. The first concerns political behaviour; the second involves prevailing difficulties of institutional effort. In this chapter we will consider compensations of a psychological nature which the Crown provides in government. The following chapter will be devoted to organizational difficulties which the Crown helps to overcome. These human factors are part of all the powers and functions of the Crown which we will subsequently examine in connection with the sovereign and her representatives. Indeed they comprise the reasons why the Crown has developed and survived over many centuries, now to be part of the democratic process in Canada.

Locating the executive power of Canada in the abstraction we call the Crown was dictated by several human problems which beset all governments. It was the problems that determined the practice, and not some ideology. Nobody planned it or adopted it; and it was not based on some "best system", "great principle", or "right thing to do". It evolved. This fact is of enormous importance. Evolution without over-dependence on ideology is a great, but unappreciated, asset in the governing of Canada, just as its opposite is one of the commonest weaknesses in the government of man.

As far as Canada is concerned, it is inappropriate to attempt to place the political system in an ideological category of some kind, such as "democratic" or "monarchal".

We should bear this in mind in determining the character of the Canadian system, or of any other system. If there is one thing above all others that weakens government and causes conflict between governments, it is the assumption that a system's political practices are primarily determined by loyalty to ideologies. They never are. Showy ideologies are invariably used as window-dressing for political reality which might not otherwise be understood, and for human actions which might not otherwise be tolerated. An atmosphere of righteousness usually surrounds emphasized ideologies, as devotees excuse any dishonesty, bigotry or crime in their cause, and engage in struggles with others who do the same. A haze of wishful thinking surrounds any governmental institutions constructed and managed according to some ideological specifications that defy human nature. Realities are neglected as people become deceived by appearance and controlled by doctrinal emotion. Thereupon ideologies fail and political structures crumble. There are other causes for failures; but the common factor in all the world's contemporary political crises and wars is the unreliability of ideologies. However grand they are in theory, however useful they may be in providing suggestions (which is their only real value), they are most dangerous as determinants of truth, bases for intergroup relations, or cornerstones of political structures.

If we can call Canada democratic today, it is not by mere profession of political faith, which is useless if it is not lived up to, but by the operation of political institutions in accordance with human aspirations and behaviour. The Canadian system can only be democratic in ideology if it is democratically workable in fact. Of the two the fact is by far the more fundamental, and it is

33

more likely to be realized if the ideology is kept quiet and unostentatious in the distant background. If we also call Canada a monarchy today it is not by profession of faith in royalty, but by the operation of the Crown as a practical political institution, and its effectiveness in a working democracy. Loyalty to the Crown was expressed in the Confederation speeches and documents in practical rather than emotional ways, while its representatives were regarded as institutions of government rather than symbols of glory or objects of reverence.* Because of this freedom from ideological bombast, democratic or monarchal, the subsequent governing of Canada has lacked much political fanaticism. There have been recent signs of such fanaticism, however, and those who encourage it should note how unsuccessful it has been elsewhere.

The Crown provides safeguards of a constitutional and psychological nature made necessary by the most uncertain element in all governments, human nature.

One problem for which the Crown is a safeguard is a tendency, inevitable in government, to worship political institutions based on ideology, and political officials for whom charisma is made to serve the same purposes that ideology does. In its extreme this tendency to worship is a form of political drunkenness always followed by a reaction, a hangover, perhaps a tragedy. Ancient tribal chiefs and modern presidents have commanded unquestioned devotion and obedience by means of it. Big public sprees during the Stuart's advocacy of the divine right of kings, Robespierre's bloody application of liberty, equality and fraternity, and Hitler's use of both ideology and charisma, are well known. But sprees of more modest proportions can and do occur, with the same emotional elements on a different scale, in the ordinary processes of government such as those of Canada. On reflection, for example, Canadians were somewhat sobered by their frenzied adulation of Mr. Diefenbaker in 1958 and Mr. Trudeau a decade later. "Mania" was the word they actually used to describe the phenomenon. They could have gone on with

---

*The title "Kingdom of Canada", which the Fathers of Confederation first wanted, was discarded by them on English advice in favour of the more religious Canadian alternative, "Dominion of Canada". Contrary to the mistaken opinion of some critics, "Dominion" never denoted domination by anyone; it referred to the biblical "He shall have dominion from sea to sea."

their mania, just as people did with Duvalier in Haiti, Franco in Spain, or Perón in Argentina, until it became controlled, as mania ultimately is, by the hero or party concerned. Or they could have replaced mania with over-confidence, and given the hero too much power to the point where they could not take it back again. But they did not. And the two prime ministers knew they would not.

We shall note many features of this situation in due course. But we should consider here, by way of example, how a seemingly fanciful "myth" may be a powerful safeguard. A prime minister in Canada (and a provincial premier) is made to know from the start of his administration that he is advising on the use of the Crown's power, not wielding power that he actually possesses. There is an enormous practical difference between these two concepts, a difference which permits and brings into play the parliamentary principles described in Chapter One as well as the emergency powers to be discussed later. However much the prime minister can do in advising on the use of power, and even though he is among the most powerful responsible heads of government in the world, he is always in the salutary democratic position of being merely a trustee–and he knows it because of frequent and colourful reminders.

But, it can be sensibly asked, are there no other safeguards that can serve this purpose? There are–parliament, the press, public opinion, a written constitution, even a leader's wife. These are all effective. But any one or all of them can lose control, as moribund parliaments, silenced presses, managed public opinion, and flouted constitutions so well indicate in many republics. As for wives, President Perón showed how to elevate by public conferment one to sainthood and another to a vice-presidency. Nor should the difficulty of providing control in a written constitution need to be cited after President Woodrow Wilson's occupancy of his high office during two years of a mentally and physically crippling illness. That relaxations of controls are easy and common and often supported at first by the people should not need illustration today. The Crown does not replace any controls. It supplements them in special ways; it is an added precaution; it may even be a "last chance".

Notwithstanding these safeguards, the tendency to political worship still remains. It cannot be suppressed. Accordingly, and again after numerous lessons, we attempt to divert such worship into harmless channels and contain it. We have learned that it is wise to keep it away from politicians because of their inclination to use it for their own benefit, and our occasional use of it as a vehicle for enthusiasm rather than judgement. We know that objects of excessive worship tend to take themselves too seriously. The simple practical fact of the matter is that democracy depends on political leaders being electable, responsible, criticizable, and removable, and worship always interferes with these needs. The Crown, on the other hand, is a harmless object for the emotions associated with worship. It was not when sovereigns were absolute monarchs; it is when they are constitutional ones. Thus we have an institution which attracts our worshipping tendencies that is advised by an institution that we should avoid worshipping.

Canadians who would declare they had no worshipping tendencies are not realistic. We are always idolizing someone or touting some fetish. All our media encourage us to do so, as do advertising and political propaganda, much of which, if we want to be frank about it, is blatantly false. Even people who only scramble to touch a celebrity or secure an autograph are engaging in a potent form of worship.

We do still another thing with our worshipping tendencies. When diverting them to the Crown we dilute them and reduce their emotional impact by changing worship into veneration. To worship is to idolize; to venerate is to consider worthy of, and to regard with deep respect and warm approval. This change is made possible by all the limitations placed on the Crown's personal representatives and by the special nature of their functions. That the change is healthy and necessary because veneration is more stable and practical than worship has often been illustrated by psychology. Man needs to venerate something in his life, and he avidly seeks worthy objects; if he does not find them he may be unhappy and cling to unnatural substitutes. In political life, where from time to time there is little enough to venerate, the Crown, above political battles, fulfills this need. In community life it provides moral leadership, especially in crisis by means of the example set by the sovereign and his family. The Crown may even be, as King Haakon of Norway proved when he stood firm against Quisling's advice to collaborate with the enemy during the Second World War, a final expression of the conscience of a people, the last hope for the moral and physical salvation of a state.

Critics of the Crown with an egalitarian approach may deplore the veneration of a sovereign who is elevated above the usual stations of life, and consider "the court" a privileged sanctum. They may also criticize heredity as being undemocratic. We shall observe later that the elevation, the privilege, and the cost are, on close examination, of little real significance as far as egalitarianism is concerned. But we should note now that in fact family and court influence are inevitable in any system, and that the sovereign and her family and court are in no more elevated or privileged a position than their counterparts elsewhere. And we should consider that heredity has not been retained for the sake of privilege, but for the practical reasons that it is one of the safest and least controversial methods of selection, and that it provides apprenticeship in a unique and difficult kind of work. Indeed, other kinds of political leaders have a choice of vocations; the monarch has none.

Comparisons in these matters are mostly in favour of the sovereign. The White House, the Elysée Palace, the Kremlin have more of the elements of a non-elected privileged court than the combinations of Buckingham Palace and 10 Downing Street, or Rideau Hall and the Prime Minister's Office. Families of presidents are influential groups in South America and Africa, and, like the Ngos in Viet Nam and the Kennedys in the United States, may rival royalty in prestige and publicity.* It is unfair, for example, to criticize Princess Margaret for performing duties at public request**, without comparing the alleged involvement of Mrs. Jomo Kenyatta in the ivory trade, and the availability for consultanships of President Nixon's brother. Enrichment of supporters and families of leaders is common in republics to an extent that has been unknown in the Queen's realms for many centuries.

Privilege abounds in communist countries; it is administrative and party privilege. Elevation has raised many presidents far above constitutional sovereigns; it is the elevation of power, perhaps strengthened by fear, and the people often have little real choice or control of them and their coteries. Political parties in many countries are full of hangers-on. "Men in grey flannel suits" who multiply in government offices may seem more demo-

---

*In an article entitled "Ready for Teddy" on June 2, 1975, *Newsweek* includes references to Mrs. Rose Kennedy as the "Queen Mother".

**As does Willie Hamilton, *My Queen and I*, London, Quartet, 1974.

cratic than aides de camp and sticks-in-waiting, but they are much more costly, often more arrogant, and almost always more conscious of privilege and protocol.* Bureaucratic red tape involves more ceremony, often more snobbery, than what is displayed in circles associated with modern constitutional monarchs. And, as Parkinson and Peter have so well indicated, much of the *raison d'être* of, and work done by, governmental and party courts offends any of the standards of judgement which critics may be tempted to apply to the Crown.

Elevation of rulers and the formation of courts and cliques are inevitable in governments of all kinds. A constitutional monarchy is not only less dangerous and costly than most of them–it also limits, although it does not prevent, this tendency to potentates and courts which neither democratic theory nor electoral practice nor egalitarianism have been able to diminish. But surely, a democrat might ask, we are living in an age which has little patience with such things. Are we? "Our age," answers one authoritative comment, "ostensibly so open and democratic, is in fact 'infinitely more exclusive, set-conscious, stand-offish and snobbish' than the assured aristocratic world of the 1840's."[2]

Another psychological problem for which the Crown is a safeguard accompanies the use of political power. Power does strange and unpredictable things to those who wield it. It affects them as alcohol does, and they vary in their ability to tolerate it. Some leaders can stand large quantities and retain their mental and moral faculties; some can bear only reasonable amounts; some get drunk on even small doses. When they react to power, some get silly, even childish, and some get arrogant, nasty and surly. Some go so far as to to misuse all their abilities and discard all their morals.

It is not only the intake of power that upsets men. Changes from one level of power to another have similar impacts. This

---

*The Hon. Judy LaMarsh, for example, on one occasion observed that a cabinet colleague "had delivered himself into the hands of a very brash and quite unscrupulous young man," and that Prime Minister Pearson "more than once commented that we would be a better Government if it were not for all the ambitious young men inhabiting the ministers' offices." "To feed their own sense of importance," she continued, "they postured that they were really 'in the know'. . .entertained lavishly at regular press parties [and]. . .vied with one another to prove they knew the most secrets."[1]

phenomenon may be called the political bends. When men go up or down through various levels of pressure in water or air, giddiness, brain damage, even death may follow. Precautions must be taken to raise or lower them in controlled ways for their own protection. A similar phenomenon of a psychological nature has been obvious everywhere in government. Some people cannot become even chairmen of committees without showing signs of it, and elevations from member of parliament to minister and from minister to head of government have often brought on acute attacks of the bends. Many procedures in public life are only explicable in terms of their control of men on the way up. And control of them on the way down is just as necessary, for the bends operate in both directions.

Any reading of political history confirms the existence of this trouble and the ease with which it occurs. Perhaps, as Lord Acton said, power tends to corrupt. If it corrupts, there is no hope of finding a remedy. If it disturbs, special constitutional arrangements may prevent the trouble, or, if prevention is difficult, render it harmless. The Crown acts as part of the necessary machinery in politics.

The difficulty, for example, of vesting in one man both the headship of state and the headship of government has been apparent, as we have already noted. The combination of pomp and power, each of which is inevitable in government, is too much. Indeed the possession of the one tends to render ineffective the operation of the other. To meet this difficulty, the Canadian constitution divides functions at the very top, deposits one set with the sovereign, and entrusts the other set to the prime minister. While the two institutions are closely associated, there is a clear line between them, and all sorts of alarms are set to go off if either party oversteps it.

Canadians are aware of these problems of power, although they will not always admit it. They can note them in other political systems. But once in a while some authority in Canada lets the political reality out of the constitutional bag. A William Aberhart will shock the country with precipitate action after quick access to power. "We have had, in my lifetime," declared a distinguished constitutional authority, "some of the weirdest and wildest provincial governments that the mind of man could conceive."[3] And, perhaps lest Canadians get too confident of their elected representatives, the mayor of their third largest municipality publicly described most of them as "political bums" who went into politics because they were not successful outside. "The politician," he is quoted as saying in a national magazine, "will do anything, absolutely anything, to get elected. He'll sell out every principle he's ever had."[4] This testimony is unusual coming from a sitting elected politician, and it invites accusations of being too sweeping. But even if it is applicable to only a proportion of politicians, it does emphasize the need for reinforcing democratic representation with safeguards against faulty exercise of power by such individuals, especially should chance send them up the political ladder and perhaps later push them back down.

The need for such safeguards is a limitation on ideologies of democracy, which tend wrongly to ignore people's weaknesses in correctly proclaiming their duties, and to elevate the advantages of representation too far above the requirements of government. Indeed these safeguards are democratic in the practical sense insofar as they facilitate the use of power in democratic government. Notwithstanding any apparent ideological inconsistency, the Crown is a democratic institution when it provides these safeguards.

A third psychological problem is a combination of lethargy and impulsiveness. Politicians and citizens are everywhere irregular in their attentions to public affairs, and unreliable in their devotion to democracy. At times they show no interest or become lulled by routine, and it then becomes difficult to arouse them to action. They may even seem not to care any more. Suddenly something happens, and interest flares up and spreads like a grass fire. Then people tend to show too much interest of a temporary nature, and society's busybodies in their trendy excitements rush to get in the way of more responsible citizens. Government and public interest in government require, however, a steady, long-term continuation of effort through cycles of calm and storm. Extremes of stagnation and sensation are not conducive to good government or to a people's happiness; indeed they can lead to the disintegration of a society.

Many political plans die as victims of public inertia. Many rights die when people take them too much for granted. And even in societies which pride themselves on being democratic and preserving rights, people confronted with suffering or wrongdoing "pass by on the other side" or avoid "getting involved". A woman, for example, may be molested in the streets in full view

40

of passers-by with no-one offering help.* Galleries of legislatures are empty during normal parliamentary business. Many political institutions function without the slightest interest of the public. Then a crisis or scandal occurs, and a great wave of temporary titillation or offended virtue rises, gathers force, sweeps along, and crashes down, ultimately to disperse in a new period of calm, but leaving behind much wreckage.

This phenomenon is a problem in political parties where it is difficult to sustain the interest of members between elections, or during elections in which not much success is anticipated. In many countries opposition parties have been out of power so long they disintegrated for lack of interest in what is an important but often dull job. And party leaders face that unfair but frequent tendency of the rank and file to select them hysterically, and then to throw on them the entire blame for lack of success, even for stupidities and mistakes for which other members were responsible. In Canada, for example, it is interesting to read the literature on the changing leadership of the Progressive Conservative party and note how rare is mention of party members' deficiencies in the prevailing concentration on the shortcomings of leaders.

Another facet of this problem of combined lethargy and impulsiveness also concerns the party system. It is the tendency of many people to neglect the difference between party activity and governmental activity. In a democracy it is not the party in power itself that constitutes the government, but members of that party, selected by its leader when he has the support of parliament. While party activity is vital in public affairs and in orderly alterations of power, there is always a danger that a party may neglect governmental responsibilities while occupying itself with seeking power or remaining in office. Indeed it may think its interests *are* the nation's interests and that pursuit of its activities *is* governing. If this difficulty goes too far in a one-party state all

---

*Public apathy can go pretty far in a democracy. When an elderly man fell and struck his head on the sidewalk in Toronto, 100 people passed by before someone stopped to help.[5] Two students at San Francisco State University conducted a revealing experiment. A girl had herself tied to a tree on a busy street and 110 cars passed before one stopped to help. A boy stayed 15 minutes tied and gagged on a park bench until the 43rd passer-by offered assistance.[6]

opposition dies. If it goes too far in a multi-party state it may be so hard to get a government at all, and the people's business may be so badly handled, that the civil service or the military feels it must assume control.

These problems of lethargy and impulsiveness are among the reasons for the rapid rise and fall of many governments in many countries–indeed for the low esteem in which government itself is often held. The tempo is too slow or too rapid. The search for messiahs and scapegoats too often displaces responsible selection and support of leaders. Party rivalry may appear to operate for the interests of parties rather than the service of the state. It is hard for democracy to survive in such a setting, because people may invoke "a plague on all your houses" and throw their support to some strong man so as to "get things done".

The Crown acts to compensate for lethargy and impulsiveness, and to ensure that as much interest as possible is directed towards governing and not just towards party politics. Canadians may desire freedom to be as lethargic and impulsive as they wish, but, nevertheless, their government must go on and their state needs their support. Party activity is important to them, but their government requires many non-partisan actions. Indeed party activities, especially opposition party activities, themselves require for their very existence many functions of a non-partisan nature. Canadians therefore make their headship of state completely free of party politics, and assign it these functions.

There are countless examples in the Canadian political system. The Crown is so non-political that Canadians, who were served by men with all kinds of backgrounds when they had Governors General from England, Scotland and Ireland, have so far confined themselves to politically independent diplomats since they began selecting their own. Lieutenant-Governors are often appointed on a political basis, but, in office, any political activity on their part is resented. This non-political role is productive. Men and women of all parties are received by the Queen and her representatives, and are thus recognized as participants in the business of the state. Non-Gaullists in France have not received such attentions from their president*, and the treatment may

---

*I once used the term "your president" in conversation with an eminent non-Gaullist politician. "He is not my president," was the reply, "he is the Gaullists' president." It was only in 1973 that President Pompidou first invited opposition representatives to dine at his official residence.[7]

elsewhere go all the way down to arrest-on-sight.

Canada has twelve people to perform numerous non-political activities of a colourful nature to relate the people to their state. And they do this day in and day out as symbols of national and provincial interest during both political doldrums and times of trouble. As we shall note later, this job cannot be performed safely by elected politicians in a democracy. As for the politicians, the Crown does them many services. For example, some members of parliament and provincial legislatures–and their wives–receive little of the recognition they feel they deserve; for them a government-house entertainment is literally the only important bright spot in their political lives. As for citizens, a telegram from the Queen or her representative to a centenarian, the laying of a cornerstone or cutting of a ribbon, the receipt of an honorary degree at a university, attendance at charity events, visits to schools, and countless other duties may singly seem mild in impact. But together they are an impressive official and nonpartisan relationship between the state and the people, at all times and not just at times when it suits the government, with all people and not just supporters of the government.

Such duties, and countless others, do not prevent lethargy and impulsiveness–they compensate for them, and often keep them from going too far. It is generally recognized, for example, that the interest of people in Canada's North was greatly enhanced during visits there by the Queen and Governors General. Indeed, politicians who previously ignored the North followed the Crown's example, but, even then, the identification of local people with Canada that they could encourage was at a much weaker level. "She did something in the North that we politicians have never been able to do," declared a Manitoba cabinet minister. "She had Tories, the steelworker, and the miners' unions, the Chamber of Commerce and the lot, working together as if they belonged to one family. If this is what having a Monarchy does, I hope we always have one."[8] As for impulsiveness, it is remarkable how regal or vice-regal attention can convey to discontented citizens that the state cares about them, even when they think the government does not. The high political temperature in the Maritime Provinces, raised from time to time by alleged neglect by Ottawa of the terms of Confederation, inevitably drops after a tour there by the Governor General. Calgary, furious with the prime minister in 1973, gave the Queen an unprecedented welcome, and the political atmosphere became noticeably less bitter,

43

until an oil crisis three months later poisoned it again. Political relations between government and citizens, among politicians, even among citizens themselves, are not always cordial, acceptable, even bearable; and people often rightly refuse to identify the interest of the government with the interest of the state. At times when people do not care or when they care too much, the Crown appears as the only existing institution which represents all the citizenry.

A further example is of enormous practical importance. Canadians may observe that in numerous republics a highly potent political force is the military, whose lethargy and impulsiveness assume too much significance in public affairs. Notable exceptions are all the constitutional monarchies. Canada has had excellent armed services in peace and war, but she does not associate military interests with political concerns. There are several reasons, and relations with the Crown are most important. We have noted that oaths of loyalty are to the Crown, not the government. By contrast, nothing deadens military initiative, raises military temperament, undermines military loyalty to the state, or encourages military intervention in politics, like oaths of allegiance to a government, to a political leader, or to the people. The Queen, not the prime minister, is commander-in-chief of all the forces. Canada is one of the few countries that has never had a general as prime minister. And any suggestion that the selection of a prime minister must have the approval of the military–a practice common in republics–would be swiftly repudiated by Canadians. Yet the army is not neglected by the state, even though military organizations tend to be sensitive about lack of attention and cause trouble. Ample sponsorship and auspices are provided by the many formal non-political military tasks performed by the Queen, Governors General and Lieutenant-Governors. Honorary colonelcies, military aides, attendance at mess dinners, the presentation of colours, and numerous other such things together constitute an impressive state recognition without any political overtones at all. These things, it must be noted, are inevitable; all states and armies have them. But the message they convey to military, government, and people is of a special national and non-political character when the medium for recognition is the Crown. It is a very different, less impressive, and often more dangerous situation when premiers present colours or ministers address mess dinners. Indeed democracy is usually dead, and the military either moribund or hyper-active, in a

44

country where the head of government's picture is displayed for purposes of honour in a barracks assembly hall.

The service of the Crown in compensating for these psychological difficulties invites comparisons with other systems. Other states arrange power at their summits in different ways. Does the Canadian arrangement, similar to those of other constitutional monarchies, meet the problems more effectively?

One fact must be noted immediately. Many monarchies and presidencies have disappeared. As far as former monarchies are concerned, the basic causes of trouble were delay in the transition from absolute monarchy to constitutional monarchy, the identification of the Crown with one side in political conflict, or the desire of politicians to consolidate their power by making themselves the symbol of the state. Sovereigns were tempted to do a little ruling when they should have only reigned. "The king can do no wrong" was not well enough established to prevent politicians from using the throne for their own purposes and, when they were wrong, bringing the king down with them when they fell. The line between possessing power and advising on its use was not clear enough. And the concept of a Crown distinct from a king was either not established or not recognized so that the supreme office was not able to survive the peccadillos of some incumbents and some prime ministers. Thus a Wilhelmina survives even wartime exile, while a Victor Emmanuel, not sufficiently detached from a Mussolini, falls. Thus an Edward VIII, regarded as an incumbent above whom is the Crown, can abdicate while the Crown continues; and a Farouk, embodying everything and ultimately embodying nothing, destroys the office when he destroys himself. Meanwhile, some monarchs remain absolute and survive. In those instances the throne may be sustained by the character and ability of the occupant. An Ibn Saud, Shah of Iran, or Hussain of Jordan can keep a throne on firm foundations for a time, and justify personal power by hard work and sensible leadership. But in the absence of a Crown in the constitutional sense, there is no guarantee that such thrones can survive incompetent monarchs and unscrupulous prime ministers.

Nor is there a guarantee that a presidency can survive more easily. Even in states with long histories of constitutional development, such as France and Germany, the nature of the presidency has altered several times with political upheavals or the changing characteristics of incumbents. The middle third of the twentieth century has seen countless variations in presidencies around the world that matched or surpassed in chaos the chequered fortunes of kings. In South America, Africa, the Middle East, and Asia, political musical chairs has been a favoured game in many presidential residences, often with death the penalty, insecurity the prize, and bad government the result. In Russia and Eastern Europe the collective head of state has often been personalized, and has changed in character with the vagaries of political power. And the American president's experience with Watergate revived the old suspicion that the combination of head of state and head of government in one man was too much, while his vice president and he disappeared in a no-more-dignified fashion than did many replaced potentates in other countries. Indeed the U.S. presidency has illustrated how the facts may belie the theories of government and the definitions of executives. "By the early 1970's," writes a distinguished U.S. authority, "the American President had become on issues of war and peace the most absolute monarch (with the possible exception of Mao Tse-tung of China) among the great powers of the world."[9]

Political worship has been obvious in republics. Russia has gone further than any modern monarchy. Outdoing Egyptian pharaohs, she has embalmed and entombed Lenin for daily display to thousands, and, following the practice of old emperors, named cities and erected memorials in honour of Stalin while he was in office, only to withdraw the homage when he died. The symbolism of monarchy is outdone in Eastern Europe where statues and pictures of party celebrities appear everywhere, and citizens are expected to buy ideological books and bric-a-brac and wear political symbols and pins. Hitler was able to get the German army to swear allegiance to him personally and the youth to organize in clubs that bore his name. Displays of Chairman Mao's photograph and circulation of his "sayings" differed little from the adulation of Chinese emperors. President Idi Amin of Uganda and President Mobutu Sese Seko of Zaire met in 1973 at the border between their countries and renamed two lakes in honour of themselves to celebrate the occasion. As one entered Cyprus Archbishop Makarios beamed down from the wall in the passport examiner's cubicle. President Papadopoulos' pictures were scarcely put up all over Greece after his coup d'état of 1973 than they had to be removed on his downfall. Argentina went further and everywhere displayed Perón and both his wives. Even such a practical politician as President Urho Kekkonen of

Finland permits his picture to appear on a postage stamp when he is in office.

With rare exceptions*, Canadians wait until politicians leave office or die before memorials are dedicated to them. They would be surprised at any suggestions for teaching Mr. St. Laurent's sayings in schools, organizing a "Diefenbaker Youth", permitting the army to swear allegiance to Mr. Pearson, displaying a living Mr. Trudeau on a stamp, or renaming the St. Lawrence after the premiers of Quebec and Ontario. Sir John A. Macdonald lies undisturbed in Cataraqui and not on display on Parliament Hill. Canadians wear no political medallions, and are forced to read no party literature. "Why, of course!" any Canadian would say. But could he be sure that, without safeguards, "such things could never happen here?"

How does the Crown prevent such practices? It acts as the repository for the decorative and emotional functions which are inevitable in any state. These functions have to be placed somewhere, and experience indicates that the less politicians can use them the better and more safely they are performed. Theoretically, it would seem more democratic to assign them to the elected representatives of the people so that the people can pay them homage. In practice, this arrangement is not democratic. Citizens in a democracy must be able to criticize and remove their representatives; indeed some of them must be in a position of not wanting these representatives in the first place and of seeking their removal in constitutional ways. Psychological factors have long been used as means for entrenching the personal powers of representatives, sometimes with ecstatic but unstable and temporary support from the people. It is safer and more democratic, therefore, to entrust the functions to the Crown. This arrangement not only puts politicians in the second place where democracy requires them to be, it also reminds them that they are servants of the state, not its masters.

This arrangement also permits a healthy political emotion among citizens. Emotion is inevitable; the need is to provide just

---

*Such as the Bennett Dam in British Columbia and the abortive "Shaw Centre" in Prince Edward Island. After the defeat of the government of Walter R. Shaw in 1966 his retiring cabinet named a new building "The Shaw Centre." One of the first acts of the new cabinet of A.B. Campbell was to rename the place "The Provincial Administration Building".

47

enough of the right kind at the right time. Otherwise emotion may become uncontrolled excitement, perhaps so intense as to become irrational, in which situation government itself becomes irrational, and public opinion, stampeded by unscrupulous propagandists, is unable to express itself at all. Constitutional monarchies have done rather well in this respect, because the emotional non-partisan functions of the Crown can be regulated, varied, and distributed widely according to the requirements of events and the needs of people.

It is sometimes said that the psychological factors should be associated with the state itself. This alternative has proved to be dangerous in both local and international affairs. It encourages extreme nationalism. Whether under a king or president, such as Emperor Wilhelm II or Chancellor Adolf Hitler, it fosters a narrow pride, a myth of superiority, a feeling of racial supremacy, perhaps even a delusion of being "God's chosen people". Citizens need loyalty to their state and devotion to its ideals, but experience indicates that they behave badly when they go too far. It also reveals how governments entrench personal powers by associating themselves with nationalistic fervour, and by assaulting the sensibilities of other states, to the ultimate ruin of a people when the fervour is revealed as collective snobbery and selfishness. Again the Crown is safer; because it is constitutional it dilutes nationalism while encouraging loyalty. "God save the Queen" is more sensible than "Deutschland über alles."

Although Canada is comparatively isolated among countries, she displays a pride that is not just inward looking, and she and her citizens are respected abroad. Nevertheless, Canadians criticize their country, and politics is one of their major national and local sports. The loyalty is strong, but it is muted and controlled. By contrast, countries with nationalistic fervours have a pride that is intense and emotional rather than substantive and practical, brittle rather than strong, reinforced by autocracy rather than public will, and characterized by chips on shoulders waiting enticingly for others to knock them off. The Middle East has long been plagued with this problem. The comparison is nothing for Canadians to be smug about—they are not wiser or more sensible than other people. They simply have the advantage of traditional psychological controls developed over centuries of experience.

We can make similar comparisons with other political systems in the effect of power on those who govern, and the consequences of lethargy and impulsiveness. South American and African politics abound with changes from benevolent intentions to autocratic domination. The loss of life from official aberrations has been enormous for a generation that considers itself "civilized," even in Asian and European countries with such long histories that it could be assumed they knew better. Much rampant power is permitted by the lethargy of citizens who cannot do much about it, or encouraged by the impulsiveness of citizens who indulge in the temporary excitements of stampedes. Meanwhile lamentably few countries have been free of explosions of uncontrolled power and public political binges. Among them are all the constitutional monarchies. It was not just that they were constitutional monarchies that brought them stability; and they were not "better" or more civilized than other countries. They had found in the Crown a practical way of handling political psychological problems of those who govern and those who are governed.

THREE

THE ORGANIZATIONAL SETTING

THE CROWN must also be considered in relation to inevitable problems of government as a large organization. We know that individuals can be conscientious or careless in arranging their personal affairs. In organizations men combine individual characteristics with others that are collective and just as unpredictable. Certain organizational problems inevitably result, and some of these have beset government with astonishing regularity and frustrated even the best intentions of officials and citizens.

One of these problems with which the Crown is associated is the difficulty in selecting an administration–a difficulty now evident in at least half the nations of the world. Countless methods have been tried. And electoral methods have included everything from sophisticated apparatus to simple shows of hands, from lofty principles to shady deals, from imposing oratory to chants of cheerleaders. Yet no system guarantees the selection of the right citizens for the right jobs at the right time. Nor has any democratic system ensured a suitable selection at all when citizens are unable to make up their minds and no party secures a mandate.

The resulting confusion is best settled in a democracy by consultations among parties and politicians. Sometimes they cannot succeed because one group will not co-operate, prima donnas may want special consideration, or necessary compromises do not go far enough to suit enough people, or go too far and weaken the ability of anyone to govern. And dishonest men will use confusion to vacillate, bribe, settle old scores, and otherwise discourage leaders and violate their electors' trust. Any idea that the trouble results from interactions of great ideas, or that the participants will all act in "statesmanlike" or "democratic" fashion is unrealistic.

Nevertheless, the country must have a government. And the longer the confusion lasts the more vulnerable its public business becomes to critics who mistakenly think the whole system has broken down, or to interventionists who might want to take over in the interest of "efficiency" or some utopia. Coups d'état are now so common they are sometimes considered a legitimate, even if illegal, method of selection. They are not democratic. They are certainly costly. And the death toll is high. This confusion can be prevented, or at least minimized, by using the service of a mediator or facilitator who is above the struggle, who has no partisan or personal interest or ambition, and who represents the whole state and its people. He may have to remind the participants of their duty to the state, as distinct from their allegiance to a faction or their interest in promoting themselves. He may have to soothe injured feelings, and resolve stubborn personal rivalries. He may be called upon to interpret rules, even remind those involved that the rules exist. But if a government that emerges is to be responsible, the facilitator cannot lay down terms, make personal choices, or order anyone to do anything. He can only smooth the way for the participants to make decisions themselves. The Crown is designed so that its personal representatives may fill this facilitating role, and secure that end for which the whole process was devised—a stable government.

The Crown is the symbol of government which remains throughout any difficulty. The existing administration may fall and the new administration might not yet be in control. But governmental authority itself remains throughout an election or a crisis because of the continuity of the Crown. The sovereign or her representative acts to secure the operation of government by encouraging the selection of an administration to carry it on. Parliament cannot do it unaided because it is locked in the political struggle. And in a democracy it is impractical for the civil service to try to secure their own masters, and dangerous for the

51

military to determine them and thereupon make them dependent on it.

It seems superfluous to cite the many instances where such breakdowns have resulted in complete chaos or in the encroachments of undemocratic practices which, invoked in the temporary emergency, remained to undermine democracy. It is unnecessary to elaborate either on how effective a Crown's role can be in crises that last for weeks, as in Belgium in 1972, or for months, as in The Netherlands in 1972 and 1973, when no parties could form a government without assisted negotiation. "I am an impartial funnel," said Queen Juliana, "gathering all recommendations which come flowing in. The object is to arrive at a solution, jointly with the usual advisers, which is the best possible reflection of the wishes of the electorate."[1] This approach during a crisis is far more democratic than the selfish jockeying of those who seek, not the electorate's wish, but their own hold on the balance of power.

If Canadian issues do not yet illustrate this apparatus effectively, we may consider one from another country*. I have heard details of several incidents which, as far as the public was concerned, illustrated how politicians composed their differences, but which were settled only after secret, strenuous, non-partisan efforts on the part of a sovereign. One typical case was described to me confidentially in 1973 by a former prime minister who considers the details so sensitive that his relevant papers are not to be made public until all the participants are dead.

His country is a stable one, but an election resulted in great bitterness among those returned to parliament, and politicians' efforts at forming a government failed. All the party leaders could agree on was to ask the sovereign to facilitate an arrangement. The sovereign talked privately with members of all parties, and got some to talk with one another who had previously not been on speaking terms. Indeed my informant confirmed how astonishing is the number of people in public life who are not on speaking terms. At length it appeared that if anyone could

---

*Canadians have had little experience with this function, although they have had some contact with the politics of the balance of power. Proportional representation and the multi-party stalemates resulting from it are not yet a feature of Canadian politics, and electoral mathematics has only come close to dead heats. But all the facilitating apparatus is on hand for use when needed. If experience elsewhere is any indication, the need will certainly come.

form a government my informant would have the best chance. He was therefore summoned by the sovereign, but, since he had already tallied the votes he could count on and found he did not have enough, he refused the invitation to form a government. In fact he thought to even try would be to jeopardize whatever chance he had. He then told the sovereign he could only accept if he had the unlikely support of a small group whose leader had not spoken to him for ten years. It was not until some time later that he learned what the sovereign did next. The other leader was invited to the palace, and, after discussion, was convinced with great skill and diplomacy that he should join the other man. Indeed he was prompted to do an even more difficult thing for him–go and offer his support instead of waiting to be asked. My informant was astonished when the old enemy called on him next morning. And other leaders in parliament were so shocked by the reconciliation that they gave aid, perhaps to see how so remarkable a combination would work. The new government lasted a normal term. But from the moment it left office the two leaders never spoke again!

My informant said that the sovereign's role in the ultimate arrangement was, and still is, unknown. Politicians would not announce how hard it was to get them to see reason–they wanted the credit for settling difficulties–and the sovereign knew his part was only as effective as it was impartial and confidential. My informant and other leaders continued to seek the help and advice of the sovereign in many subsequent difficulties which government and parliament could not settle. He emphasized that the value of this help lay in its being non-partisan and representative of the entire state and all the people. After describing several instances, he concluded: "I'll bet the professors can't tell you that!" Sure enough, the following day a professor of constitutional law solemnly assured me that the sovereign had played no role in the formation of governments and in settling other difficulties. An opposition statesman later gave me still more instances of valuable royal participations which politicians on his side had encouraged when in office.

I asked the two former prime ministers whether a constitutional president* could perform this function as well as a sovereign. Both said no because they felt his previous political

---

*A constitutional president exercises powers similar to those of a constitutional monarch, as opposed to an executive president, who exercises powers directly assigned to him by the constitution.

affiliation would be a handicap. If he had been of the government party, especially if he owed his post to the support of its leader, he would have to be a most unusual man to talk effectively with other parties. The situation might be more difficult if he had opposed the government. They thought his worst handicap would be the temptation of a former politician to relish his power and act too directly, something a sovereign is rarely inclined to do.

Personal antagonism among politicians in Canada was well illustrated by John A. Macdonald and George Brown, who only came together after much rivalry for the sake of Confederation in which they both believed, and severed personal relations as soon as it was achieved. And there are instances, such as the animosity between Mackenzie King and Arthur Meighen, which affect the operation of parliament, and which illustrate how difficult a necessary reconciliation can be. Fortunately such relationships have not gone dangerously far–yet.

Another way the Crown compensates for collective difficulties concerns the removing of ministers. When men wield power they are generally loathe to give it up. Private citizens may also show similar reluctance: some are difficult to dismiss when found wanting; some are unwilling to retire; some cannot understand the need for relinquishing parental control when their children grow up. Mackenzie King even followed a very dubious expedient of remaining in the prime ministership over three months after his successor had been selected. Further afield, leaders have clung to office in such manner as to weaken governments, perhaps even to invite the turmoil of forced removal, and others held on so well they became immovable.

Because Canadian heads of government do not possess personally the powers of government, the powers are not endangered when they leave office. They cannot say, as so many desperate men have done, that their presence is necessary for the continued operation of the constitution. The transition between administrations is therefore smooth, and they can retire, later to die peacefully in their beds. Thus did all eleven governments change leaders, some long entrenched, in the period 1966-72. This orderly change is not standard procedure in the twentieth century.

Instances where representatives of a Crown have directly aided the retirement of a government or of a member of it rarely become public knowledge. They occur, nevertheless, in several ways. The most drastic concerns a government that defies a par-

54

liament by controlling, by-passing, or even destroying it. The resulting upheaval may be so great or the manoeuvre so successful that neither the Crown not any other institution can do much about it. But even here the Crown can try, especially in wartime, to rally support for constitutional government in the face of an administration that has lost control, that has too much control, or that is about to capitulate to an enemy. We have already noted King Haakon of Norway as an example. The more usual and much less spectacular instance involves a leader who cannot be told his usefulness is over. In theory a party may always dismiss him, or make things so hard for him that he has to go. In practice this is most difficult. In the case of the "grand old man", party members may not want to "break his heart". They may not want a sure winner of elections to go, even though they know he should. And they may fear his wrath and be frightened of telling him. For example, how can a party remove a Roosevelt or a Stalin? As for lesser members of government, there are instances when the leader is too gentle or cautious to remove a colleague himself and carries on or seeks someone else to do the job for him. Not everyone wants to incur Harold Macmillan's title of "Mac the Knife".

It is surprising how readily the help of a head of state can be asked. Direct dismissal by him is only rarely recommended in the most abnormal circumstances, and he would certainly not invoke it if asked privately to do it on his own. And yet it was necessary for President Radhakrishnan of India to refuse the astonishing request of Prime Minister Nehru that the President write Nehru asking him to dismiss Krishna Menon.[2] More frequent is the secret request by members of a government that the head of state exercise, not a dismissal power, but a persuasive power on a minister against whom they would not want to take action. This action cannot be threatening or forcing if the Crown's help were asked; the minister could rightly charge interference and his colleagues could not take responsibility. But, as we shall see in a later chapter, it is an effective action if well handled.

The third organizational difficulty for which the Crown compensates is the problem of providing advice–a problem which is troublesome in every political system. Indeed, neglect of this problem is one of the weaknesses of democracy, and has been the cause of much turmoil in many republics. The conventional theoretical wisdom assures magic flows of informed advice from people to government and back again, among officials carefully located in an administrative hierarchy, and from what is to some the fountain of all democratic knowledge, the committee. This procedure may result in more open decision-making, but as a practical consequence, it can serve only that part of the advice-giving function concerned with fact-finding and opinions. But fact-finding and opinion, usually conflicting, must ultimately result in decision-making, and the latter is dependent on something more complicated than facts and opinion–the taking of responsibility. Buck-passing, that prevailing limitation on democracy, stops with the prime minister.

Few citizens realize the awesome responsibility of a prime minister and the loneliness of his job. Surrounded by advisers, but advisers who disagree, pressured by interest groups, including selfish ones, and supported by colleagues, many of whom put a price on their support, he soon finds that there are few advisers whom he can trust, and that frank, disinterested, honest, and confidential advice is a rare commodity. Indeed he may himself be a difficult person to advise–there are people in all walks of life with this weakness–and to influence him at all may even be impossible as the power, self-confidence, vanity and ambition so common at the summit tempt him to consider himself infallible and indispensable.

For a prime minister in a country with a constitutional sovereign, the latter is a remarkable official with useful experience which no-one else can command. Born and trained to the job, he is usually acquainted with public men throughout the world, privy to what goes on behind the scenes in government, informed on the successes and mistakes of countless officials, knowledgeable on public issues and how they are handled, informed on public opinion, completely independent of politics, and without ambition for higher office because there is none. He has no political responsibility. His power is almost always wielded on advice. He must use his experience in constitutional rather than absolute fashion. From such an official a prime minister can get informed opinion which he can accept or reject as he wishes with no obligation whatever. "The Queen", writes a contemporary observer, "is perhaps the best informed person in the country. But she is more than that: she is the most experienced of them all in public life, bearing in mind her long continuing role as governments come and go, her unbroken reading of state papers, and her personal knowledge of virtually everyone of political consequence at home and abroad. . .In short, the Queen is a very accomplished political person."[3]

Prime ministers confide in and consult their own colleagues and advisers to whatever extent they are able and willing to do it. From the sovereign they get another viewpoint. The mere fact there are such discussions at the highest level makes heads of government more careful about doubtful decisions and more confident about troublesome ones. This process has often gone so far that a prime minister, worried about some risky policy that has only barely won consent in cabinet, returns from a talk with a sovereign with some new suggestion that no-one thought of before. This happens often in the early stages of a new administration.* But even in experienced governments it is common for a prime minister to ask for and get from a sovereign or his representative, not just suggestions, but encouragement to rethink a policy with which neither prime minister nor cabinet was really satisfied. And this consultation can be most useful in the dying days of an administration when ministers tend to be careless in making decisions which they do not have to implement, or hesitant about solving problems which they would prefer to leave for their successors. Furthermore, it is also common for ministers, pushed by a powerful prime minister into halfhearted agreement, to encourage the chief to try an idea on the sovereign.

The consultation may also involve a warning. Everyone needs an occasional warning, but few can warn anyone else and get away with it. If that person should be a prime minister he may badly need a warning and not get it, because either no-one

---

*For example, some new premiers, wary about appearing too dependent on civil servants, especially after long tenures of office by their defeated opponents, have found able sovereigns (and the able among their representatives) to be useful guides, in a general way and on large matters, to the requirements of power. Even if a premier does not seek guidance or the representative of the Crown does not give it, encouragement is often needed and readily given. Citizens and colleagues do not usually regard a victorious premier fresh from the polls as needing such assurances. He is the man of the hour with a popular mandate. But it is then that he often needs encouragement the most, especially if he is taking office for the first time. And he may need it even more six months later when his "honeymoon period" is over.

will give it or he will not be receptive to it. Many leaders have fallen because they did not hear or heed advice they did not want. "My experience," said Bonar Law on the fall of Asquith and Lloyd George, "is that all Prime Ministers suffer by suppression. Their friends do not tell them the truth; they tell them what they want to hear".[4] The warning apparatus of a constitutional monarchy serves to reduce this difficulty in major non-partisan matters by means of discretion and sensitivity. Indeed prime ministers, even powerful ones, have sometimes deliberately encouraged sovereigns to give frank advice because they knew they needed it.

This process goes still further. A troubled prime minister may be able to "let his hair down" only with a sovereign. Like any other citizen, he may need someone with whom to talk things over, especially someone who will not gossip afterwards. Anyone can test the significance of this service by asking himself how many relatives, friends, and colleagues he has to whom he could unburden himself in time of great trouble, and from whom he could secure wise and confidential sympathy, judgement, and support. Prime ministers are often in this position, especially in crisis, and it is sensible for a state to provide him with this kind of help at his own level of power.

Could not this service be provided by a constitutional president? It can and it is in some countries. But it is not nearly as effective in the hands of such a figure. In the first place, constitutional presidents have not achieved the symbolism and identity with the state that the sovereign has, and, with the exception of a few especially distinguished personalities, they have had far less experience in this kind of role. In the second place, a prime minister will rarely share his confidence with a president who is an ex-politician to the extent he will with a sovereign, especially if the president was once an opponent or one of his own subordinates.

It must not be supposed that a helpful sovereign stands ready to offer his opinions when he thinks a prime minister needs them. It is the prime minister who advises the sovereign when and how to exercise his authority, expresses the opinions, and takes the responsibility. But the mere fact the prime minister does this encourages him to brief the sovereign and prompts an exchange of opinion. There is a great difference between these direct and indirect methods. The direct one would be intolerable in responsible government. The indirect one maintains requirements but permits realities.

This is a modern interpretation of what Walter Bagehot considered in outlining the sovereign's three rights–the right to be consulted, the right to encourage, and the right to warn. Today they are not so much rights which the sovereign automatically possesses, as opportunities which the sovereign is in a unique position to provide.

This fact is largely unknown to the public, even to most government officials. No prime minister will indicate how a sovereign helps him. Nor can the sovereign say a word about it in a constitutional monarchy where the prime minister is responsible. As for officials, even ministers, it is only a rare one that knows what goes on when a prime minister talks to a sovereign. Indeed it is remarkable how few ministers are in practice privy to their prime minister's secrets and have his trust, despite the theories of collegiality associated with cabinet government. "You see," said Prime Minister Stanley Baldwin, "there are only three or four people whom I can take into my complete confidence and trust them never to say anything outside."[5] One has only to interview several ex-members of a cabinet to find how common this situation is. I have encountered many instances in several countries where a prime minister regarded his sovereign's advice as wiser and more practical than that of any minister, and as more informed in respect to public opinion. And I have also encountered many ministers in whom their prime ministers had no confidence at all.

This process also operates in Canada at the level of Governor General and Lieutenant-Governor. We will examine the details later. We must note here, however, that it operates in different ways, according to the personalities and experiences of incumbents, and if, when, and how the opportunities described are put to practical advantage. The advantage is no less valuable in both national and provincial government in Canada. And it is no less misunderstood. I recently enquired in a provincial government about the premier's consultations with the Lieutenant-Governor. I learned that the two men met regularly, and that the premier relied much on the Lieutenant-Governor's great experience and common sense. Yet one senior official was unaware that they had met except on formal occasions–a situation which is both sensible and correct.

Theorists may claim that this kind of influence by the sovereign is undemocratic because he or she is not elected, and criticize it because it is secret. I consider this attitude to be undemocratic. It places too much faith in the virtues of election, and election is not infallible. The sovereign must be non-partisan; election tends to give a head of state a partisan image and thereby fragments the public support he should have. Nevertheless, the sovereign (or his representative) is responsible because he acts on the advice of representatives of the people. And ministers may ask for, take, or reject the sovereign's advice as they wish. As for secrecy, the sovereign must act secretly if politicians are to take responsibility, and if the kinds of issues he may be asked to give advice on are to be settled. In all the instances cited the sovereign acts on behalf of the people when other institutions cannot do so. Sometimes he even has to remind politicians of *their* responsibility to the people. Indeed the experience of this century indicates that democracy has little to fear and much help to expect from a constitutional sovereign, but a great deal to dread from arbitrary and careless elected governments. As for other sources of advice, it is no more "democratic" for a prime minister to consult his wife, an executive assistant, a party official, a "dollar-a-year man", or either of the two persons so evident today–the "special envoy" and the "faceless bureaucrat". Even elected politicians are not necessarily democratic or responsible in giving advice, when a prime minister knows they are motivated by purely partisan, sectional, or personal motives, as distinct from the interest of the people as a whole.

There is a fourth general organizational difficulty for which the Crown is designed to compensate. People tend to be suspicious of large organizations, however much they need them, and require some public relations, colour, spectacle, and especially personalization, to show, among other things, that organizations are human. The needs of individuality resist those of collectivity. Examples are legion in Canada and everywhere else. We need only to cite Canadian banks which now use symbols, cocktail parties, and even scenic cheques for glamorous payment of bills, in attempts to relate to the needs and emotions of customers. ("Commerce 'O Canada' Cheques", proclaimed the Canadian Imperial Bank of Commerce with mellifluous artistry, "make cheque writing a beautiful Canadian experience.") It is difficult to think of one function that is performed by organizations in our society without decoration and personalization of some kind.

Government is not an exception. Every system in the world must try to make itself look well. It has to, because governing and administering can be dull to officials and citizens without something to relieve the monotony and improve the appearance. There is danger, however, in encouraging too much appearance and not enough work. In a constitutional monarchy, therefore, appearance tends to be neglected in the civil service, encouraged in the government only to the extent that public relations are necessary in the electoral and legislative processes, and promoted at the level of the Crown to add a general colour and human interest to government. For people who cannot buy soap without a movie star promoting it, or go to church on Easter Sunday without a new hat, it is sensible to provide in government some official auspices or cosmetics to hide unpleasantness, make impressions, encourage loyalty, and humanize institutions. Princess Anne's wedding was just as relevant in government as a university convocation, an Oscar night, a firemen's ball, or a child's birthday party. Without these, how dull the world would be!

And how twisted in its priorities! "One half the human race at least," said Walter Bagehot in a famous statement, "care fifty times more for a marriage than a ministry." And they are right, especially when 500 million of them around the world watched and enjoyed a spectacular, low-cost royal wedding at a time when the United States was presenting the expensive Watergate affair and the shame of a vice president, Chile featured the violent death of its president, Greece entertained mankind with another episode in its continuing political tragedy, and the Middle East provided war and an energy shortage. The wedding was human life writ large and well staged; the other events were shabby, costly, governmental failures. It is a tragedy of politics that there is not enough of the first to compensate for the impact of the second.

This is the organizational side of the decorative functions already mentioned in connection with psychological needs. Mere utility is not enough to attract attention and regard. A government must also appear useful. And its inevitable blemishes must have some compensations. If it can arouse interest and enthusiasm, even cause laughter from time to time, its usefulness is increased because people will forgive it more and condemn it less. No matter how efficient it is, a government, no less than an individual, suffers from being too serious, especially when it fails. It also suffers from not being serious enough, and a certain amount

61

of dedication and ceremony are necessary to counterbalance some of its frivolous aspects. This counterbalancing is the key to the matter. Some lumps in public throats are just as powerful in the civil associations of a people as some ballots in a box. But too much makeup in the wrong place may destroy appearance and mislead judgement.

The Crown in a constitutional monarchy permits much of this counterbalancing. It provides a restrained constitutional makeup to improve the appearance of the whole government, without the garish display that has so often brought down absolute monarchies and republics. Some display is inevitable. The Crown provides it to prevent obvious alternatives. "I think that public opinion today likes a certain amount of pageantry", said Mr. Clement Attlee, during a parliamentary discussion on revenue for the Queen. "It is a great mistake to make government too dull. That I think was the fault of the German Republic after the First World War. . .the trouble was that they let the devil get all the best tunes."[6]

A government must also look well and seem efficient to people within its official hierarchy, including its armed services, civil service, party structures, and even its ministry. If dull routine is too obvious many of these participants do not feel part of a thriving, living organization. If frivolity is too prevalent they will feel unworthy. Mischief results from extremes of both. No matter how well or ill the business is being done, officials, including the opposition, must feel that something is going on that justifies their careers. This is particularly true in huge organizations where an individual or small group may feel irrelevant. When administrations fall, even when systems die, it is often clear that the organization did a good administrative job, but the people in it did not believe it and did little or nothing to prevent its demise.

It is to the top that officials look for appearance, and they will not forgive its absence despite even the most efficient work of the leaders. One need only consider what professors and students want of a university president to understand the point. They expect him to lead, but, no matter how well he does it, they also require him to represent them, entertain them, conduct their public relations, and appear interested in everything from their research to their athletics. "I have never been inside his house" or "we never see him at football games" are common expressions of injured dignity or reproach among professors and students that tend to overshadow the president's successful efforts at promoting a budget or developing a new faculty. As far as government is concerned, the old idea of bread and circuses is well known. Even in the process of law, justice must not only be done but also must seem to be done. Often it is officials closest to authority who, with respect to appearance, are impatient, resentful, perhaps even ashamed of their government. It is fascinating to observe when one visits governments in other countries the attitudes of officials to their leaders. Regardless of efficiency, these attitudes range all the way from loyal pride to absolute contempt, and the spirit of government is affected accordingly. A sad alternative is so often followed: when a political leader's appearance fades he tends to resort to shock tactics from autocracy to belligerency to war to gain approval from his colleagues and public attention for himself. His people pay a high price.

Government is not greatly disturbed by appearance-making in a constitutional monarchy. Constitutional cosmetics are applied more generously, more expensively, and with much less effect, in many republics than in the monarchies. The difference between the two systems parallels the difference between the institutions at the top that are accentuated. In constitutional monarchies it is the appearance of the Crown that is emphasized, that is the symbol of the state, its traditions, and its people at the higher, non-political, and continuing level. The whole people, the government, and the opposition can respond to this appearance. In most republics it is the government of the day or government-sponsored activities that are emphasized. The politics of that government and the characteristics of its members and leaders, both of them political and temporary, then intrude on the appearance of the state, often to besmirch it. And a people, a succeeding government, and certainly an opposition cannot respond continuously and effectively. In the one system the soul of the nation is emphasized, in the other merely the fact of a government.

The difference is therefore not just one of appearance, but also one of feeling among citizens for a whole society. In a constitutional monarchy the system encourages a sense of belonging to the state as a family with benevolent parents and independent children. An absolute monarchy or absolute presidency of any kind demands a relationship like that between overbearing parents and obedient children. A colourless republic tends to foster the atmosphere of an orphanage: there are officials and services, but only limited identity.

As for costs it is not difficult to assess them, but very easy to misinterpret them. The constitutional sovereign, as we shall note later, is actually an inexpensive institution performing functions which have to be performed anyway at a fraction of what it would cost the government to do the same thing, and at a pittance compared to what citizens pay to have their votes solicited, their commodities packaged, their patronage enticed, and their desires stimulated.* In republics, by contrast, constitutional presidents cost a little more with less return; the head-of-state roles of executive presidents cost much more. For the latter category the costs in terms of huge staffs, spectacular political displays, monuments and propaganda of many kinds, and perhaps marching political armies, assassinated opponents, and banished citizens, almost unknown in constitutional monarchies, have reached scandalous proportions.** "All forms of government have their advantages and disadvantages," said King Gustaf VI Adolf of Sweden. "But you are not likely to get one that costs less than a monarchy."[10] I interviewed a former Scandinavian prime minister who had a private study done and found his sovereign the least expensive head of state in Europe.[11]

Behind the colour, entertainment, and formality are other

---

*A citizen pays annually for his constitutional monarchy less than he spends to have himself coaxed into buying a particular breakfast cereal. The "promotional sales" of Kelloggs Corn Flakes, for example, are reported as costing 2.3 cents for each 12 ounces package.[7] The gross cost to the people of Britain of the Queen, royal family, civil list, palaces, travel, and other expense is approximately 11 cents per person per year, and most of that is spent, not on the sovereign's needs, but on public duties.[8] Even this cost is misleading because (a) sovereigns have turned over much family wealth to the state; (b) people and the government ask the sovereign to perform services for them and expect her to pay the expense, and (c) countless people and organizations make money from the various activities of the Queen and the royal family. In 1971, for example, Lord Aberdare, Minister of State for Health and Social Security, reported to parliament that in 19 years the Queen had turned over to the state incomes totalling more than £38 million more than she received from the Civil List, and the Crown Estate Commission paid taxes of over £7 million.

**Even the cost of the American president surprised many U.S. taxpayers in 1973. Some members of Congress calculated it as more than $50 million a year, while an official of the Office of Management and Budget estimated it as more than $100 million a year.[9]

less desirable, but inevitable, elements for which a Crown's decorative functions help to provide some necessary compensation in government. These are snobbery, social climbing, petty ambition for status, and the like. Indeed critics sometimes condemn them as features of crown activities. Actually they are features of government of all kinds, and they bedevil all political institutions. They are also evident in all other large organizations. The socialite who flutters among the teacups, the scion of an "old family" who demands the entrée, certain clergymen and church authorities who everywhere avidly seek preferential status, and the do-gooders who scramble for invitations, are just one category of a breed that includes all who fawn at the seats of power, vie for a government's patronage, use political parties for selfish advantage, or assiduously promote themselves up a bureaucratic pecking order. The snob and climber are obvious in all parliaments and political parties, in fact wherever someone wields power or commands patronage, and in no less numbers in republics than in monarchies. Indeed it is not difficult to assert that they swarm more busily in the governments of many republics.

Anyway they will swarm. The Crown provides a bright light in government that attracts some of them and gives them harmless satisfactions. Were they to depend on other institutions, already beset by people like them, their antics would not be harmless. If, for example, they had to "scramble" in the House of Commons, noted King George V, when he was Duke of York and studied Bagehot, "the number of social adventurers there would be incalculably more numerous and indefinitely more eager."[12] When parliaments fall, such people are always part of the cause. Indeed the lack of a harmless method of attraction may be a reason so many political parties fail outside the Commonwealth; powerful selfseekers thrive in their inner sanctums, and influential hangers-on and pseudo-intellectuals in them present poor images to the public. Actually such people are only a small proportion of all the persons involved in crown activities; looking after them is a comparatively minor function; and it is wrong to consider them a privileged court. They are better described as inevitable prima donnas who are invited occasionally to preen themselves on a harmless perch to keep as many of them as possible from roosting with their counterparts elsewhere.

Occasionally the term "frivolity" is used to describe some decorative funtions. To use it smacks of puritanism, which is dangerous in government. In the first place, man is frivolous in many

65

ways, in all political systems, and he wants to be silly and trifling at times. He may eagerly touch a celebrity or brag that he has met a potentate, and it is wiser to enable him to do such things through harmless yet patriotic deference to a spectacular but constitutional head of state than through the forced adulation of an autocratic head of government or the slavish touting of an exclusive ideology. Political frivolity is inevitable everywhere; by any comparison it is harmless in the monarchies. Free people may bow and sing anthems to a monarch, while they can criticize and oppose a prime minister. Under many presidents people must do what they are told, pay homage, and shut up.

In the second place, it is good for political man to be frivolous from time to time. Real danger occurs when he is too serious, especially when he is trifling, silly, even selfish in his seriousness. Then he becomes stuffy, quarrelsome, short-sighted, and hard to get along with. Governments behave the same way when they succumb to puritanism in their relations with citizens and other governments. Unfortunately puritanism then becomes fashionable and eats away at the very foundations of a society. Anything that lightens public life, from parade to party, and gives people a chance to celebrate harmlessly something or someone is a relief, a diversion, perhaps even good fun. Where too much colour is removed from public life, obsessive efforts to be over-serious frustrate our ability to communicate with one another and prevent many political institutions from working properly. The drab results are everywhere obvious. The decorative functions are not frivolous. They serve serious purposes. But if our reaction to some of them should be considered frivolous, that is all to the good because we are behaving naturally. It is time society became more inclined to throw its collective hats in the air, and had more chance to shout "hurrah!"

As for democracy, the glory of a constitutional monarch as a person is not the result of the appearance of the Crown. Nor is any theory of egalitarianism weakened by his status. Power, money, raiment, ceremony, and entertainment mean no more to him than the daily work and equipment of any citizen. Reigning is his job, and it is tough, monotonous, continuous, tiring, with long hours, both on display when he must always look his best and appear interested, and at his desk where he is imprisoned by paperwork. His money is spent for public purposes at the public's request. He cannot retire, look for an easier job, or complain to a union like other people. He is expected to do his duty, and that duty is not to himself but to the state. When, on the other hand, politicians dress up the government by dressing up themselves and their offices, they tend to delight in their own glory and that of their regimes to the point, as we have noted, where citizens cannot do very much with them except to tolerate them or plot their overthrow in what is always a costly and undemocratic convulsion. The constitutional sovereign lives and works hard in respectable comfort, and his prime minister–unlike many presidents–takes office, relinquishes it, and dies without being hated. As for egalitarianism, the status of the sovereign encourages it by lessening the extent to which politicians with power inevitably seek status for themselves. Indeed, egalitarianism today is weakest in many republics where political privilege makes a mockery of it. The examples are, again, numerous and obvious, and they give substance to the recent assertion of so practical a publication as *The Economist* that "the pageant of royalty is now in its most useful generation. Republics are dangerously out of date."[13]

The Crown has often been used to meet a problem in external relations. It is everywhere difficult for governments to present a suitable image to other governments and peoples in other countries. Prime ministers are rarely appreciated outside their own countries. A people may not understand how unknown their government is abroad, or how uninteresting, perhaps distasteful, their leaders may appear to other governments. And they may not know that their own image to the world is affected by that of their government, or that a series of temporary politicians may not succeed in giving them any image at all. Their government in other eyes represents not them or their country but their politics, which others may or may not like. And in a democracy the opposition rightly must throw mud at the government's image, and the mud shows in international relations. Presidents and sovereigns with power share this difficulty with prime ministers. Constitutional presidents are better off, but for only short periods of time. Constitutional monarchs are in the best position of all because, with longer terms, and unsplashed with political mud, they are able to project better an image of their countries. Queen Juliana has projected The Netherlands to the world better than all the Dutch prime ministers; President Nixon's world image as head of state was not indicative of American democracy; heads of state in eastern Europe present visages of bureaucracy, not of national character; Idi Amin's antics do not put Uganda in a favourable light; many South American presidents enhance the image of "banana republic". As for prime ministers, their images are weaker because they are temporary and partisan, and because most countries know little and care less about the politics of other countries with which they want to be friendly.

Canada is a good example. Her image abroad is clear. Nobody knows or cares much about her politics and government, even her next-door neighbour. Nevertheless, some Canadians who have doubts about Canadian identity repeat the old mistake of thinking it depends on political image, and they encourage an unjustifiable inferiority complex. "It is stuff and nonsense," wrote General Vanier, "for us to talk like some half-baked intellectuals do. . . .To show how highly regarded Canadians are abroad, I could have said: 'If I had to travel through many countries in the five continents and were given the choice of a passport I would say: A Canadian one'."[14] This happy respect does not result from the government's image abroad–it has no image abroad–but from how people see Canada as a state. To foreigners, Canada's political, psychological, and organizational settings present a rational and stable appearance, and Canadians enjoy a good political life. At home, Canadians may take the appearance for granted, and neglect the practical aspects of governing that lie behind it, many of which are provided by the Crown.

FOUR

THE QUEEN OF CANADA

ELIZABETH II is the personal expression of the Crown of Canada, is Queen of Canada, and is a constitutional monarch. It is this combination that explains her role as head of state and as an institution of government.

It is the Queen of Canada that we are concerned with in this book. I have not presented additional facts about the Queen of Great Britain, of Australia, or of any other of her realms, and have omitted constitutional issues and examples which do not involve the Queen of Canada. The sovereign's role in Canada has been constitutional, legal, symbolic, and psychological. Because of distance, she and her predecessors have not played the direct part in the details of Canadian government that she does in Britain, such as maintaining continuous contact with prime ministers and regularly being consulted, advising, and warning. In Canada her representatives are responsible for this direct contact.

We note immediately that the Queen plays the same role in some other parts of the Commonwealth, and we face the question of a shared Crown and head of state. What is the advantage in modern times of this arrangement? And does it limit or compromise the sovereignty of Canada as an independent nation? We must first examine briefly these questions before carrying our discussion to the internal operations of the Crown in Canada.

The Commonwealth serves 850 million people, and includes huge nations and tiny states. Of its 33 members, all recognize the Queen as Head of the Commonwealth. Sixteen new states plus India are republics with their own heads of state distinct from the Queen; eleven, including Canada, are monarchies with the Queen as head of state; and five, all new states, are monarchies with monarchs other than the Queen as head of state. Much has been written and said about the Commonwealth. In this discussion we must confine our attention to three of its attributes which answer the questions we have raised as they concern the government of Canada.

The international attribute has two aspects. One is well known. Canada and other similar members are included in a fellowship that has been most difficult to establish and maintain in the world, an association of nations. Its supporters regard the Commonwealth as a valued example of international friendship and cooperation in the interest of world peace. It may seem a loose association, but a Canadian visiting another member country on the opposite side of the world does feel a family relationship which associates him with the other people. Even if the association is no closer than that with a third cousin in individual life, the feeling of being related is both pleasant and practical. Any benefits, however intangible, are to be appreciated in contemporary desperate attempts to recognize a family of man. And these benefits can be most practical to a country like Canada that depends so much on international relations. "I fully believe," wrote L.B. Pearson, "that there are sound, practical reasons for continuing our association quite apart from sentiment. I could not imagine anything more valuable than an association based on the old British Commonwealth which would permit members from the emerging continents of Africa and Asia to share with Britain, Australia, New Zealand, and ourselves a multilateral, multiracial association. I thought that this might be a very useful piece of international machinery, as indeed it has turned out to be."[1]

The second international aspect is rarely appreciated, although it is one of Canada's greatest assets. We might call it the integrity of transition to nationhood. Over the centuries nations have conquered other nations and developed lands into colonies.

But they have rarely been inclined either to give up easily the fruits of their conquest and development, or to admit accusations of exploitation. Governments and citizens are proud in such matters. The gaining of nationhood by dependencies has usually required a long process of negotiation, perhaps rebellion, and the aftermath may be bitter. As far as Britain's original dependencies were concerned, there were struggles, but in the separations from the control of the mother country there was a stage which permitted a gradual, peaceful, and face-saving change–independence under the Crown. It facilitated independence by encouraging enthusiasts to demand change and diehards to relinquish control without "losing face", and enabled a family association to remain. The British learned the lesson when their American colonies broke away, and since then have followed a natural process comparable to the experience of any citizen who grows beyond dependence on his parents, becomes able to support himself and handle his own affairs, and maintains an independent family relationship. Other empires disintegrated, leaving little friendship either among the parts or between them and the original mother country. This kind of change may be compared with existing situations in eastern Europe and Asia, where countries that are independent in name but dependent in reality have too close an association, not simply with another country, but with the government of another country. In these cases, such as Hungary vis-à-vis Russia, and Tibet vis-à-vis China, the discontents of the dominated meet the tenacity of the dominating with obvious friction and pressure.

Canada was able to weaken and then sever all governmental connections with Britain until she had complete control of her own affairs. Colonial status changed to dominion status and then to independent status, when conditions in Canada justified the change. The existence of the Crown permitted face-saving on both sides. The provinces early got all the trappings, symbols, and ceremonies to make them appear grown-up, even when they had little else to justify their identities. And the government of the mother country saved face every time it gave up some power because the old links appeared at first to remain. But the old links did not remain, and, when everyone realized it on both sides of the Atlantic, the Crown became the symbol, not of colonialism, but of nationhood. In contrast, the last two decades have dramatized in many new states how the heat and passion of ab-

71

rupt premature independence without stability have compromised sovereignty by rendering a state unbelievable and its people unhappy.

There has been nothing unbelievable about Canada's independence under the Crown and in the Commonwealth. And the legitimacy of its governments, all eleven of them, has never once been questioned. This unappreciated fact is important. Canadians have argued over the exercise of constitutional powers and over some governmental institutions, and have taken their politics with intense seriousness. But they have not had any experience, so common among republics, of questioning the legality either of governments or of political power itself. Even their provincial governments, each with a representative of the Crown to reinforce its identity, have never had to face extinction at the hands of the central government. There is not even a provision, like India's emergency presidential power, by which the central government can adminster a provincial one. Not only has the sovereignty of Canada been strengthened by the Crown's auspices, but the sovereignty of the provinces in their own spheres has been firmly established. This is no mean asset for democratic federalism.

But cannot these arrangements be legislated? They can. Legislation may be changed, however, or honoured in the breach rather than in the observance; and even whole constitutions can be altered, as they have been in numerous countries, in assaults on the system. Sovereignty, rights, and powers do not tend to last if they are just entrenched; they must also be enshrined.

The second attribute of the Crown in the Commonwealth follows from this enshrining of sovereignty, rights, and power. It is the comparison with the trust and the benchmark described in Chapter One. We noted that the Crown is like a trust in which powers are kept for safekeeping; or like a point in the constitution, beyond both sovereign and government, from which powers are created, measured, and controlled. In these respects the Crown is not Britain or some person, document, or ideology. Rather it is a tradition encompassing all the political and legal experience of centuries of trial and error. It is not, however, a glorification of the past. It is a political instinct, as ethereal, but also as practical, as other natural instincts of man. And it shows up in practice. A prime minister does not resign or ask for a dissolution of parliament upon losing the confidence of a parliament because the procedure is set down, or because he thinks it is the democratic thing to do. Other heads of government have shown how easy it is to get around such requirements. Rather, a prime minister is made aware of his duty by tradition that developed the procedure as the sensible and natural thing to do.

When Canada shares the Crown with other members of the Commonwealth she is sharing this tradition. She has not tossed it out and attempted to start anew and learn the business of government all over again. Once more we should examine by comparing. Much of the trouble in new nations is similar to what would happen if a horse tried to act like a lion. Their governments too often ignore the instincts of their people, and, as a result, political fact bears little resemblance to constitutional form. Even old states may have the same trouble. Greece lost her ancient democratic instincts with resulting chaos. Similarly, in Russia, tsardom and imperialism are as evident today as they were in 1900 because they were not permitted to assume democratic characteristics. Some other countries are trying to develop democracy on the basis of autocratic traditions or vice versa. And many of them are unable to maintain political institutions because they have no recognized traditions on which to base them, make them work, and command continuing public support. Under the Crown of the Commonwealth the tradition was continued and allowed to develop as the member countries matured. Rule by certain autocrats, for example, was not terminated abruptly and carried on by other autocrats–it changed gradually to the constitutional democracy to which experience brought it.

Autocrats still pop up in Canada, and many political peccadilloes spice her public life. But they are recognizable and controllable in front of the backdrop of tradition and instinct. Canada could withstand even Duplessis, Hepburn, and Aberhart at the same time. We try some practices, recognize they are not sensible and drop them, because we are able to drop them. Other practices we recognize as sensible, and retain them. We are able to make changes without a tenacious past, a rigid document, or a dominating ideology to hold us down. Always the Crown encourages both tradition and change. This is not the fashionable view, which tends to concentrate on the tradition but not on the change. Nevertheless countries with governments under the Crown are able to make changes far more readily than most republics. And tradition enables them to do it effectively because the change can be measured against the collective traditional wisdom which is, after all, the most natural test. The contrast is sharp with states that are governed on the basis of what some single group at some period of time wrote down as the rules; or on a series of contemporary experiences which, rooted in nothing, cannot survive the passing phenomena which gave rise to them; or on some unsuitable practice or ideology which the constitution was not flexible enough to reject without disaster.

The Crown has therefore turned out to be democratic in the most fundamental sense of the word. Those who favour more "practical" or "democratic" arrangements are really being impractical and undemocratic if they neglect the question: who is to make the arrangements? Will it be one group of contemporaries with their inevitably limited experience, interests, and ideas? Or will it be all the people of a state over a long period of time? History has shown that no generation of citizens alone can speak for a nation. Human nature rejects such arrogance, as it is today rejecting it in many countries. The Crown permits continuing or discarding the political experience of its citizens garnered over many centuries, accommodates contemporary experience, and then presents the sum to future citizens in such a condition that they can add to it or change it as their times dictate. This view of democracy is wider and more natural than the conventional one. In addition to the advantages discussed in Chapter One, it interprets "the government" and "the people" as a continuing, co-operating succession of generations.

This view also permits some compensation for one of the great limitations on democracy which it shares with all systems. It may be impossible for the will of the people, their institutions, and their officials to prevail, no matter how carefully it is planned and stated. It may be obstructed by forces of which they have no control, or mistakes which can neither be avoided nor blamed on a particular group or action. The idea that a democracy, any more than other systems, can always be in control of its destiny is wrong. It is here too that tradition aids contemporaries in making democracy work. Like instinct, it may automatically give warning of unseen danger that has struck before, or it may suggest suitable actions on the basis of earlier experience. It may therefore provide some readiness for meeting the unexpected, and a little needed immunity against that old problem of politics so obvious today–man's tendency to repeat again and again his worst mistakes.

The third attribute of the Crown in the Commonwealth is its compensation for the psychological and organizational problems described in Chapters Two and Three. Every nation has these problems; and when it comes to political behaviour there is nothing unique to Canada. The Crown in Canada provides the same compensations that it does elsewhere, and we shall examine the Canadian practice later. We adopted them because they have worked, as a scientist does when he accepts existing techniques and then proceeds to build on them by improving them and adding his own. There is nothing old-fashioned or limiting about this practice; neither sovereignty nor integrity is compromised. The problems must be met.

We should now examine the Crown in Canada itself, and ask first how it was established and how it developed.

The Queen represents, among other things, the origin and growth of government. The system developed over the centuries in a gradual way already described in Chapter One*. Setting up this system in the colonies was like putting a jet engine in a farm wagon. Tiny Prince Edward Island, for example, was assigned in 1769 a Governor and a Lieutenant-Governor, and all the trappings of government for 271 inhabitants. Conditions in all the colonies were primitive; most officials were not very competent; there was little money, and the home government had to pay the bills or sponsor bond issues; and the people at first cared little about handling public business when they had all they could do to keep alive. The resulting politics appear quaint now. But they were important then, and they changed as the colonies developed and their people gained political experience. And the colonies

---

*In Canada, the powers of the Crown developed from the establishment of the older colonies which later became provinces. Several of their first constitutions were created by royal prerogative which enabled the sovereign to establish colonies without action by parliament. This prerogative, which is the total of powers accumulated over centuries of government and still remaining with the sovereign, thus transferred to Canada a system of practices and institutions already developed, tried, and accepted. This system was set forth in the prerogative instruments to early governors, which were the letters-patent, which established the governorships; the sovereign's commission, which assigned the powers to the governors; and the instructions, which gave detailed orders. "This the King's Commission", wrote Thomas Pownal, a famous colonial governor, "becomes the known, established constitution of that province which hath been established on it, and whose laws, courts, and whole frame of legislature and judicature are founded on it: It is the charter of that province."[2]

got the official status which served as a mark of sovereignty which they desperately needed to provide legitimacy, and which remained as a constitutional umbrella until they grew to maturity.

In the midst of this transition, even before the colonies were politically stable, this shared heritage helped to bring three of them together as four provinces in 1867, when they had little else in common besides allegiance to the Crown. They set up, on their own initiative and terms, another, central system, with the same structure they had known for so long. Then the new structure developed further on a national scale, and the system was continued or set up in six new provinces. Meanwhile the constitution remained stable in a century when constitutions elsewhere were created and destroyed in reckless fashion, until now Canada's government is one of the oldest in the world, and, as we have noted, her people have enjoyed, by global standards, a remarkable freedom from real political trouble. All this did not take place because Canadians were superior people. They had a system that transplanted well to their environment, and then worked.

The Crown ultimately took a new position, in a kind of outer political space. It was beyond both the sovereign and the British government. As Canada became an independent nation, she retained the Crown as her governmental tradition while relinquishing one by one all her constitutional ties with the British government until she now has none at all, except the process of amending the British North America Act. This function the British parliament still handles on Canadian initiative and advice, and it remains only because Canadians have been unable to agree on how to replace it. Thus did Canada become, in the words of Prime Minister St. Laurent, "an autonomous state, subject in no phase of its domestic or external affairs to any other authority than this Canadian Parliament."[3] Like any lasting physical structure, this system was erected, not on haphazard contemporary guesswork, but on carefully calculated measurements from the tradition, in much the same way construction workers measure from a benchmark. And when they learned how, Canadians made those measurements themselves–not the British government.

If this arrangement sounds theoretical, we can appreciate it in a practical way by a contrast. Russia, eastern Europe, and China have a common and comparatively new source of political measurement–Marxism. The system measured and constructed from it has been transplanted. But the measuring was done, and is still being done, by the Russian government; and the latter's symbols, officials, soldiers, and party workers are evident in the countries of Eastern Europe, with inevitable limitations on the sovereignty of those countries and clashes with their older traditions. If those countries are thwarted in attempts to throw off or modify the limitations, China, on the other hand, is in a position to complain and act. What she is doing is developing her own political system with Marxism as an ideological tradition, wanting to do it herself, and protesting the identification of the tradition with the Russian government. Had Russia kept her Tsar, made him a constitutional monarch, and then adopted communism, Marxism might have been better served in some form of commonwealth of independent communist countries!

Where does the Queen now fit into the Canadian constitutional system? Again we can refer to measurement from the political tradition. It is not enough to have a symbol of the tradition; men always want someone to personalize it, to be a reminder of it, perhaps even be an assurance of its continued benefits. In every country from Sweden to Haiti, from Argentina to Japan, even, as we shall see, in some provinces of Canada, personalized symbolism has existed in some form. And not just in politics; religion, commerce, entertainment require it too.

But there is much more to the matter than that. The exercise of constitutional powers requires a reference to something that indicates the sources of the powers. Lawyers, for example, who uphold land claims in court go far back to original sources of land grants for justification of their clients' rights. Governments themselves may measure their jurisdictions in constitutional difficulties by citing centuries of precedents. And people generally use the same kind of reference as recognition and reinforcement of civil rights. In such matters the power is all at hand in Canada, and the justifications and precedents establish it with the minimum of doubt and controversy. The Crown, and the Queen as a fixed visible representative of it, constitute a stout foundation for this arrangement. By contrast, countless legal processes have been chaotic in many republics because the source of power was not sufficiently identified and preserved. In many of them traditions have been destroyed, nothing substantial has taken their place, public life has no stable foundation, and human rights are treated with tragic carelessness. For example, a common mistake is to make a dominant president the symbol

77

from which all power is measured (and some presidents have cultivated this recognition with enthusiasm); chaos may follow his death or overthrow. The guarantees afforded by parliaments, parties, and laws have been as readily swept away. The unthinkable has happened so often in twentieth century governments that an institution and an individual representing a thousand years of rights and powers constitute a strong base for law and rights, and valuable tradition for political action.

The person, name and titles of the Queen are used frequently in Canada as reminders of fundamental constitutional principles. But phrases like "my people", "my government", and "in the Queen's name"; and designations like "royal commission" or "Queen's Bench" do not mean that she rules. She is the personification of the processes of government. When she does things on the advice of her ministers, either directly or through her representatives, it simply means they are working from their visible source of tradition and authority.

We must now ask who the Queen is, and why we have this particular kind of head of state to identify the Crown. In any system it is easy to define a sovereign, president, or collective head of state in a constitution, and assign powers and duties to him or it. It is much harder to determine how to get the kind of person the office requires. It is also easy to ignore the difficulty by saying that all power comes from the people and they can decide who their leader is, what he should do, and how he can be made responsible to them and be changed by them. That the problem is more difficult than the theories of leadership indicate is illustrated by many dramatic and often tragic careers of republican heads of state and heads of government. And these careers have been agitated or doomed as much by the inability of citizens to control them as by the weaknesses of the officials themselves.

The sovereign of Canada is selected by automatically accepting the eldest son of the previous sovereign, or, where there is no son, the eldest daughter, or, where there are no children, the nearest heir in a collateral line. Canada is not thereby choosing the sovereign of England to be, *ipso facto*, her sovereign. That person actually occupies several separate jobs, being sovereign, separately, of each of the nations that so acknowledge him or her. It is a simple and understandable process, and, except only in rare instances, it is one that causes no dispute about succession and no interruptions between reigns. And it is not just a matter of heredity. The parliament of each of the states may consent to or alter as it wishes the procedure by which the throne is occupied, the succession, and the powers and titles of the sovereign. Any citizen can appreciate this arrangement who has been president of several organizations at the same time.

Both the advantages and disadvantages of accepting the particular person are obvious. In the first place an heir is usually well trained for the job, is accustomed to the rarefied atmosphere in which a head of state lives, carries forward the accumulated experience of a reigning family, has a wide acquaintance among officials, knows his constitutional place and the practical implications of what he can and cannot do, and remains in office long enough to make a personal impact. Furthermore citizens hear much about him, and, contrary to general opinion, modern sovereigns who were obvious heirs have met more citizens and learned more about public business before taking office than most other officials of government. Heredity permits apprenticeship. In the second place, disadvantages may appear when the ordinary transfer from parent to child is disrupted by death or abdication so that a minor or unexpected heir ascends the throne, when the heir suffers from personal deficiencies, or when the method is opposed by some who want a public choice in the recognition of a head of state. These disadvantages may also appear in other methods of selection.

Canada's six sovereigns since Confederation, with the exception of Edward VIII, who reigned for less than a year, have ascended the throne as adults, were experienced in public life, enjoyed a wide acquaintance among world statesmen, remained in office long enough to make personal impacts, and established a reputation for integrity and service. Prior to the present reign the sovereign was a remote head of state because of difficulties of communication, and it was not until 1939 that a reigning sovereign first set foot on Canadian soil. Members of the royal family did come on visits and several occupied the post of Governor General. Nevertheless, the link between the sovereign and the Canadian people was strong, even in the absence of personal contact. This contact came in the present reign with improved communication. The Queen's activities are seen on television, and royal tours have taken her to every part of Canada.

We must consider whether or not the impact of the monarchy and its *mystique* are weakened in Canada by the fact of an "absentee monarch". However distinguished the sovereign, and however greatly her personal contact with Canada is increasing, is

79

the personalization of the Crown effective enough on Canadian soil among Canadian people? In one respect, not having our own sovereign who is exclusively Canadian, the answer is "No". In all other respects the answer is that both the impact and *mystique* are greater in government and among the citizenry in Canada than are the impact and *mystique* of the constitutional heads of state in the republics. Indeed one of the main reasons for the decline of democracy in many republics is the fact that their heads of state may have no impact or *mystique* whatever, while their heads of government have far too much of both. In this respect Canada is fortunate.

The matter gives concern to some Canadians. This concern is recent, and is based on periodic upsurges of nationalism, unfounded suspicion of alleged relics of colonialism or British domination, feelings that a head of state should be a resident, or simply on blaming the Crown as a convenient scapegoat for weaknesses that were not its fault. But the matter goes beyond these concerns, and involves the practical operation of government. Opinions and facts must be considered in relation to Canada, but, if they are to be really relevant to Canada, they must also be considered in relation to governing. That this dual obligation is essential is illustrated by many countries where its neglect resulted in rejection of institutions or complete chaos.

How easy it is to forget this obligation was shown by the Special Joint Committee of the Senate and of the House of Commons on the Constitution of Canada which reported in 1972. Some witnesses feared that changes in the present "head of state system" would imperil parliamentary government. Whereupon the Committee observed that "a number of Commonwealth countries have become republics without undermining their parliamentary systems. Consequently, there seems to be no basis for the fear that the substance of our democratic institutions, and the basis of our responsible government, would be affected by any change in the relationship of the head of state to the executive and parliamentary institutions in the country." Such a change, it concluded, would be one of style, not of substance.[4]

The committee's dismissal of the matter is totally inadequate in view of the facts. A study of the Commonwealth countries which became republics indicates how parliamentary government can be changed: Bangladesh, Botswana, Cyprus, The Gambia, Ghana, Guyana, India, Kenya, Malawi, Nauru, Nigeria, Sierra Leone, Singapore, Sri Lanka, Tanzania, Uganda, and

Zambia. Canadians would scarcely consider all their parliaments adequate or cabinets effective, or regard the prevalent military influence as desirable. Nor would they approve of India's state system. Nor would they think of their head of state in terms of Archbishop Makarios, President Idi Amin, President Kenyatta, or General Gowan. They would not consider their prime minister in relation to Mrs. Bandaranaike or Lee Kuan Yew, or permit the abolition of their prime minister altogether, as several of these states have done. As for "the substance of our democratic institutions," Canadians would not desire the press censorship that prevails in most of these and in many other republics.[5]

By any comparison, a change in the relationship between the head of state and the parliamentary institutions is one both of style and substance. Indeed the change in substance has everywhere been greater than that of style because the facts of politics belie appearance. The head of state or the prime minister often becomes too powerful or too weak; legislatures frequently become rubber stamps; oppositions often disappear or are ignored; and associations between citizens and their government become greatly altered. These consequences can be noted in countries cited by the Committee. And they go pretty far. Prime Minister Indira Gandhi dramatically displayed them in June, 1975, when her government arrested hundreds of political opponents and imposed nation-wide censorship following demands for her resignation after a court had convicted her of electoral offences. In the same period, President Idi Amin was indicating again to the world how little human rights counted in Uganda by condemning a writer to death for calling him "a village tyrant" in an unpublished manuscript. Even more spectacular politics were meanwhile being featured in Bangladesh after Prime Minister Mujibur Rahman made himself president of a one-party state with consequences that would make any parliamentary committee shudder.

The reason for such upheavals is too often obvious. The tradition of political instincts dies, and there is little to hold institutions together, or to prevent men from raiding one another's powers and interpreting the constitution to suit themselves. In this respect the Parliamentary Committee was like the builders of Thor Hayerdahl's famous first reed boat, the "Ra", who, when copying ancient designs, omitted a tension cable because they thought it a decoration, and found in mid-Atlantic that its real purpose was to keep the deck from sinking.

Monarchal traditions are strong among Canadians. The French and English heritages are full of them, and many "new Canadians" carried them from countries which had them for centuries. There is nothing alien about monarchy in Canada. And, what is more important, Canadians would be unable to shake it off under republicanism to the extent they have already modified it. If the sovereign were removed the characteristics of monarchy would be assumed by other institutions of government such as heads of state, heads of government, and powerful political parties, and they would not likely be as constitutional and democratic. This process has happened in many parts of the world, as we have noted, and there is no indication Canadians could avoid it. The reason why it happens has already been described–people tend to think only of the styles and titles of monarchy, and neglect the fact that monarchal ways of governing may continue or arise without them.

It is therefore unrealistic for Canadians to consider their democratic apparatus compromised by a constitutional sovereign. As for compromised nationalism, there is not a shred of evidence that the national identity of Canada or any other similar members of the Commonwealth is any less strong internally or externally than that of other countries. The evidence is the opposite in many republics, including the members of the Commonwealth that became republics. Indeed it is realistic to understand that the sovereign and her representatives are often the only political institutions that convince foreigners that Canada is not a copy of the United States. Most important of all, however, is the fact that the Queen, as a combination of several sovereigns of independent states, demonstrates a means of sharing identity so necessary to human communications without destroying the proud, conflicting, and troublesome demands of sovereignty. This is a goal that regionalists and internationalists have long sought. In the light of history, and contemporary politics, the Queen's present role may yet prove one of man's great political inventions.

The Queen is not, of course, unique in Canada as a shared institution. Many businesses, labour unions, churches, sects, societies, and political parties share leaders with counterparts elsewhere. Indeed they often go further and share policies with absentees, and even take instructions from them.

Having a sovereign reside in a country is an asset. He and his family are seen; his home may be a landmark; he has close contact with the government. There are other factors, though, and they become obvious when in this respect the Queen of Canada is compared with other kinds of head of state.

We have noted that the visibility of a constitutional president is often limited compared to that of the Queen. He may be a colourless figure or old-time politician whom citizens make little effort to see. He is rarely spectacular enough to represent the state, and often he has little symbolism. Most of his time is spent in a capital city, and his travels to other parts of a country are limited by a short term of office. He is sometimes very old and unable to travel much. Those who opposed him in a presidential election may not pay him respect in office. In some states, and because he is relatively colourless, his activities are actually confined by the government which prefers to use the state's public relations for its own purposes, or by a prime minister who does not wish to be overshadowed. In all respects except one–regular weekly contact with the government–the Queen has the advantage in Canada. She is so colourful that everything she does makes news. She has travelled throughout the country, and most Canadians have met or seen her. And our constitution, for practical and democratic reasons already described, deliberately assigns her the public relations of the state and instructs her to overshadow the prime minister, and this she can properly do much better than any constitutional president.

Admittedly this is a personal judgement, but, on visiting many republics, I was impressed by the fact that so few citizens know much about their constitutional president or have even seen him. As for other kinds of presidents, the impacts of many are so great that the headship of government displaces the headship of state with resulting detriment to the state and limitation of democracy. In the United States the comparison is valid, because the impact of the president as head of government tends to overshadow his impact as head of state, while the latter interferes with his responsibility as head of government. Even if we consider the Queen alone, her impact as head of state is very high by any comparison. But she is not alone. Eleven governors have among their functions the representation of the Queen in their jurisdictions, and this representation in turn enhances their status and symbolism. Their presence combined with her auspices and periodic appearances make a formidable and practical expression of the constitutional headship of state which is surpassed by no republic.

Comparisons with republics should involve, not just the impact of the headship of state, but also the actual actions of the head of state and the kind of practices which arise under his type of jurisdiction. Practices that are acceptable in the United States and France but not in Canada are indicated elsewhere in this book. Other republics provide more striking examples.

Juntas and military presidents in South America and the instability of regimes and the violation of rights in that continent are well known. "Third world" countries, often one-party states, have included practices in their administrations which may or may not be necessary in the local context, but which are certainly not compatible with Canadian practice. There are numerous examples of this. In Senegal the prime minister is really a chief executive officer to the president, and the latter presides over the cabinet.* Nigeria, which has both a Supreme Military Council and a Federal Executive Council under a general as president, illustrates an arrangement found in several African states, where continuing administrative services co-exist with a party organization that sponsored a revolution or engineered a coup on a winner-take-all basis. Keeping a balance between the resulting large structures is a major task. The rights of citizens in countries of central Africa are linked with governments, perhaps even with a president, and not with some non-political institution. East African presidents tend to run one-man administrations and gather to themselves the charismatic and decorative aspects of government. They are also hard to criticize and remove. The status of some, like Nyerere in Tanzania and Kenyatta in Kenya, invites the question, applicable to many presidents, of what will happen when they die or leave office. The lack of a recognized opposition is everywhere obvious.

Practices and events in older states also present numerous questions for republicans. Indonesia adopted federalism in 1946 and abolished it in 1950. In 1960 President Sukarno empowered himself by decree to control political parties, even to dissolve them. Franco reigns and rules in Spain, and has himself chosen to be succeeded by a king. Portugal had fifty political parties within two weeks of its "liberation" of 1974. In Finland a prime minister can be an acting president. In eastern Europe heads of

*The association of republican governments in West Africa with France is closer now than Canadian governmental relations with France or Britain have been since colonial days. There are some sixty thousand French civil servants in the Ivory Coast.

state sit in councils of state, a practice Canadian governments long ago discarded, and may act as party secretaries, something Canadians have never permitted. In Switzerland the presidency rotates in turn every year among members of a seven-man council, a unique system workable for special local reasons only in Switzerland. Uruguay tried the same practice in a nine-man group from 1951 to 1966, and, as even Swiss authorities predicted, it failed. In mainland China musical chairs describes the location of power at the top. Duvalier of Haiti became president for life and secured the succession for his son. Chiang Kai-shek was president in Taiwan while his son Chiang Ching-kuo was prime minister; at one time the vice president was also prime minister. Closer to home Robert Kennedy was appointed attorney general by his brother President John F. Kennedy, a situation Canadians vigorously protested in the days of the "family compacts". Indeed in every type of presidency there are practices which Canadians attracted to republican forms must consider. To advocate them for their virtues without making allowances for their defects, or for the need to adjust even their virtues to the Canadian environment and make them work, is the height of folly.

It would be speculating to claim or deny, on the basis of Canadian experience, that the headship of state would have more or less impact if the Governor General alone were made head of state, or some other kind of official were created for the purpose. (Only a sovereign who inherited the Queen's role as personification of the Crown would be comparable.) But experience elsewhere indicates that His Excellency would have a difficult time. Even just the difference in *mystique* would present problems. It can be illustrated in some ways by comparing the Moderator of the United Church of Canada and the Cardinal Primate of the Roman Catholic Church. They serve the same purpose, but one has international auspices that give him the far greater *mystique* and resulting impact. Even Canadian politicians indicate the difference; if the two clerics are at an official function in Ottawa it is the cardinal who gets the most attention; in provincial capitals a bishop easily outshines a president of a ministerial association. The difference would be even more apparent at the governors' level. Most citizens, who do not know the Lieutenant-Governor's connection with the Governor General, would, in the absence of the Queen's auspices, regard him more as an agent of Ottawa than the personification of that headship of the province which, in a local parliamentary and cabinet system, is as essential to democracy as its counterpart at the national level. Furthermore, we may be unable to avoid a weakness of many republican heads of state that prevents them from making a sufficient impact after election and during a short term. The Governor General as a representative of the Queen is in fact a more impressive official than most constitutional presidents because of the symbolism; and yet there is enough symbolism left over for the ten Lieutenant-Governors to care for their needs and to keep their premiers democratic.

This last point is the most important of all. By any comparison Canada's eleven legislatures and first ministers are immensely powerful, yet are also controllable. And the controls of the legislatures and executives on each other are usually strong. The nature of the Crown, and the kind of emphasis on it provided by the Queen and eleven representatives, contribute greatly to this situation. This fact, often missed in theoretical discussions about republics, is readily recognized by comparisons. The prime ministership is an example. There is no prime minister in the United States, and many executive problems result from the president being in effect his own prime minister. In France the prime minister is not a real head of government in Canadian terms—he can even be dismissed by the president for his own reasons—and the national assembly does not enjoy the power of the Canadian parliament. In eastern Europe a prime minister is only comparable if he is also first secretary of the communist party, and then he is more powerful and less responsible than Canadians would tolerate. In most other republics the prime ministership—if there is one at all—is new, and its incumbent varies from an executive assistant to a president to a powerful autocrat. Many of them foster the rubber stamp theory in legislatures, while others have so little control that their legislatures are in a continuing state of chaos. Furthermore, Canadians have been able to keep prime ministers, premiers, and ministries in office for long periods of time, much longer than most countries can permit, without either endangering government or identifying it with one man or group.

There are other reasons for all this variation, but the one that appears common in all comparisons is the existence, or lack of it, of a sufficiently colourful entity that represents the state and the whole people, both contemporarily and traditionally, and is above and detached from the partisan affiliations of executives and legislatures. If this entity is not visible or effective enough, the other institutions have difficulty controlling one another and serving the state and its people. This weakness is not a problem in Canadian government. The Queen is obvious but not oppressively obvious. The Governor General has enough prestige to be respected, but not enough to interfere in government. The two together provide a spectacular headship of state which is detached from both politics and administration. Within this system the prime minister, and the premiers too, are among the most powerful and responsible heads of government in the world. It is the Queen who enhances this power and responsibility. The reason is subtle, but most practical. Just as it is an advantage to the people and to parliament to have the prime minister wield power but not possess it, so is it an advantage to the prime minister to have a Governor General who has the functions and auspices of a head of state without being one. Many republican prime ministers have good reason to wish for such a practical arrangement.*

And yet the Queen's colour, impact, and international association have enabled all political power to be exercised in Canada. The Queen now exercises only one exclusive power in respect of Canada, that of appointing a Governor General, which she can only exercise on the advice of the Canadian prime minister. Long ago the sovereign exercised many powers on the advice of the British government. As responsible government developed in the new nation after Confederation, the British government increasingly consulted Canadian authorities before advising the sovereign on Canadian matters. Later the Canadian government periodically advised the sovereign directly until it took over the function and the British government relinquished its role entirely. Meanwhile the sovereign from time to time empowered the Governor General to act in certain matters without any reference to the throne at all. The sovereign continued to do this until he exercised, on Canadian advice, only those prerogative powers

---

*This practicality is often neglected by critics who may consider such a governmental process to be "rigmarole", because it does not seem sufficiently identifiable, explainable, firm, and strong. A general of the Hitler regime, in which ideology and decree supposedly made all matters of government clear, was reputed to have chided an Englishman on this subject. "We surround our constitution with bands of iron; you encircle yours with moonbeams." "Perhaps so," was the reply. "But can you cut moonbeams?"

involving granting of honours and performing international acts. Finally, while retaining on Canadian advice his ability to exercise these last powers, the sovereign also enabled the Governor General to exercise them too, leaving the Canadian government to decide whether it would advise the sovereign or the Governor General to exercise them. This gradual transfer of powers ended in 1947 with new letters-patent for the Governor General proclaiming that "we do hereby authorize and empower Our Governor General, with the advice of Our Privy Council for Canada, or of any members thereof or individually, as the case requires, to exercise all powers and authorities lawfully belonging to Us in respect of Canada." This document was approved by King George VI, not as King of England or any other country, but as King of Canada. And it was countersigned by the prime minister of Canada.

One question bothered some Canadians for a while. Why, they asked, could not the Governor General represent Canada on visits abroad as a head of state? He can. Among "all powers and authorities" of the sovereign in the letters-patent is the duty to represent Canada abroad, and this duty was transferred to the Governor General along with the others. If, therefore, he visits another country, he is representing Canada, not the Queen, and is doing it in no less constitutional fashion than heads of state elsewhere do in respect to their countries. As far as protocol is concerned, the matter is now being recognized following Governor General Michener's visits to The Netherlands and Iran, just as nations have had to recognize recently the fact of collective headships of state in communist countries and give status to visiting party secretaries. This contemporary development is one more effective gradual change in the Crown, a change that has now made it a symbol, not of colonialism, but of nationhood.

The form and reality are therefore both perfectly clear. The Crown's powers have all been placed as far as the Queen is concerned in a permanent and unbreakable trust in the hands of the Governor General of Canada, to be exercised at the discretion and on the advice of the Canadian government. She lends her name to the trust, but the trust is Canadian. Thus the powers of the head of state are now completely in Canadian hands.[6]

Legitimacy of power, uncommon among new states, and often unstable in old ones, is one of Canada's most valuable assets at both federal and provincial levels. It is this legitimacy, and the stability which usually accompanies it, that the Crown provides to make democratic and republican principles work in Canada. "What we've got," said Mr. Michener of the result, "is a unique democracy, which has not only all the elements of other, republican, forms of democracy, but has the additional features which are given by an institution, the Crown, of great antiquity and authority, established and proven over generations, supported by that experience and by a certain amount of ceremony and perhaps a bit of mystique."[7] To personalize and strengthen all this, the Queen serves in an impressive position with colourful and practical results.

FIVE

A TEAM OF GOVERNORS

THE TEAM which represents the Crown within Canada is an ingenious set of officials. Spectacular enough to keep eleven powerful governments in second place, and yet not get in the way, they preserve a balanced constitutional position supported by the requirements of parliamentary government. They have mandates which are highly democratic. They cost very little and save the taxpayers money. On the whole, however, Canadians do not know what this team does.

There is nothing remarkable about this situation. Most citizens in any country, whether monarchy or presidency, know little about the functions of their constitutional headship of state. The reason is simple in Canada. The governments cannot inform us; and the eleven officials can speak only in what Lord Tweedsmuir called "governor generalities". Their powers and many of their functions, like those of their cabinets, can only be exercised, in democratic theory and actual practice, secretly, behind the scenes, and in an atmosphere of trust. The people who work out front are the politicians, and the responsibility we place on them puts them at the centre of the political stage. Hyperactive or politically vocal governors would be a sign that the wrong actors were speaking the lines. Nevertheless, it must be difficult for governors who perform essential functions to hear occasionally the question "what do they do?"

That there are eleven members in Canada is an important fact about this team. The Governor General, as we have noted, is not head of state, but he exercises all the powers of the Queen who is head of state. The ten Lieutenant-Governors are federal officers appointed by the Governor General on the advice of the cabinet acting on the recommendation of the prime minister, at salaries fixed by the parliament of Canada. But they are also heads of provinces occupying the same position relative to provincial governments that the Governor General holds in the federal sphere. This dual role keeps them from being mere local agents. Because executive power in Canada is still vested in the Queen, although not wielded by her, and Lieutenant-Governors are appointed by means of it, and because the provinces possess sovereignty over their own powers, the Lieutenant-Governors are as much representatives of the Queen in provincial government as the Governor General is in national government.[1] This arrangement, we have stated, is a practical aspect of federalism. It relates the provincial governments directly to the Crown in their jurisdictions, and brings to provincial constitutions all the traditions and practices of the Crown described earlier. The sovereignty of provincial governments is therefore specifically and directly designated. It is not passed on to them either by the parliament of Canada, which has not the power to do it in a federal system, or by the Governor General, who is not himself a source of supreme power of his own, and who heads a government which is sovereign only in federal matters. The constitutional status of the provinces is therefore greatly enhanced by the practice of keeping the Crown and headship of state separate from the Governor General.

To citizens all this may seem constitutional gymnastics. But let them get into legal difficulty and they soon learn what crown auspices mean in the provinces. Cases concerning liquor regulations and insurance, problems of getting a divorce, differences over grants to education, questions of civil rights–have highlighted the facts of federalism in Canada, among which is the Crown's role in preserving it at both national and local levels. Even a premier may try to invoke the idea, as Mr. Bourassa did in extraordinary fashion in October 1973, when he pleaded executive privilege on declining to appear in court because "the premier is invested with rights and privileges of the Crown."[2]

The governors are at the top of their governmental jurisdictions, and, for reasons described earlier, the ministers are their ministers. A few politicians may get impatient with this arrangement, and when they do they usually reveal why it is necessary. Some are not inclined to enjoy being upstaged, like Mackenzie King, who was irritated when Governor General Athlone acted as head of state at the Quebec Conference of 1944, and like Maurice Duplessis, who treated Lieutenant-Governor Onésime Gagnon with an open rudeness that was matched only by Mitchell Hepburn's attitude to Lieutenant-Governor Herbert Bruce. And they will invariably act in such circumstances as if democracy were their exclusive prerogative. This attitude is exactly what the existence of the team of governors is designed to discourage. Elected politicians should be upstaged constitutionally. It is ominous and undemocratic, for example, when a Maurice Duplessis changes a protective formula. "It will sound odd, won't it," asked one of his ministers, "when we hear Onésime reading the Speech from the Throne and saying 'my government'!" "I've thought of that already," replied Duplessis, from whose cabinet the Lieutenant-Governor had been appointed. "This year the speech reads '*the* government' not '*my* government'." After Mr. Gagnon was sworn in while guests were drinking his health, the premier turned to him and said: "Lieutenant-Governor, go to the devil!"[3] Incidents like this are fortunately rare in Canada. But when premiers consider themselves first citizens, they soon surround themselves with protective devices against the operation of democracy, and may ultimately tell other institutions to "go to the devil". They then become autocrats or they fall. Indeed their secondary position in Canada may protect them from themselves and their governments from them. And this may well be a reason why Canadians can tolerate for so long a Smallwood, Angus L. Macdonald, Duplessis, King, Manning, or a W.A.C. Bennett. We held on to them longer than most other democratic states do their premiers, knowing we could get at them when we wished, while they could not change the constitution to their advantage, however powerful they became.

One of the worst mistakes citizens can make in assessing their governors is to consider prime ministerial autocracy democratic because a majority of them voted for the prime minister, and governors undemocratic because they are appointed. Experience has indicated that democracy has more to fear from prime ministers than from governors. Canada's Edward Blake warned of this fact a century ago. "It is very well to tell the people that they are all-powerful", he said, "but if they hand over to a Cabinet inordinate powers, not susceptible of being kept under control, they may be deprived of the free expression of the popular will which is necessary to popular government."[4] "The notion," wrote Dr. Forsey, "that a people can vote away its liberties is an affront to common sense. It is not democracy but demagogic heresy".[5] Canada has already had an obvious share of undemocratic government, especially in the provinces, and it is fortunate that her several dictators have had to soar on clipped wings. One of the surest indicators of trouble, of which citizens should be immediately suspicious, is the use by a premier of the term "my government".

How important is this arrangement is illustrated in republics where heads of government were able to take over the headship of state, often professing that democracy required their elevation. Even the Germans, with the recent example of Hitler behind them, only with difficulty convinced Conrad Adenauer to confine himself to the chancellorship rather than follow de Gaulle's tactic of moving to the presidency and literally taking the prime ministership with him. And the Greek government removed its king in 1973 in the interest of "democracy"; the head of government took over the top job and became an absolute monarch in fact; strenuous but unsuccessful efforts were then made to define the headship of government again; while the president by his actions invited the coup d'état that removed him and his prime minister. It is not difficult to recall several Canadian premiers who would have done similar things if they could. Such incidents may be exciting for some politicians, but they are invariably difficult and costly for the citizens.

These two basic principles of Canadian government, the sovereignty of the provinces in their spheres and the democratic secondary positions of first ministers, are clearly established by the existence of the team of governors. But that is all. The federal and provincial governments are not run by these men, and, except in the most abnormal circumstances, they are not expected to interfere with other institutions. The first ministers have full executive responsibility, and are answerable to their legislatures and electors, not to the governors. The legislatures have full parliamentary powers and privileges, and the will of each is sovereign in its own sphere. As for the citizens, the governors have no control over them and are not responsible to them. The requirements of every tenet of democracy are met by this arrangement.

But, as earlier chapters have indicated, there is far more to the effective operation of government than what is obvious on the surface or what is suggested in theory. What there is for the governors falls into three categories: the functions which reinforce, yet make responsible, the executive, particularly the prime minister, which we will include in Chapter Six; and the emergency and decorative functions which we will examine in Chapters Seven and Eight.

We must now consider the men who hold the offices of Governor General and Lieutenant-Governor.

One thing is clear about the effectiveness of the Crown in Canada–much depends on the calibre of the governors. The exercise of all the powers and functions can be smooth and useful if the right men are appointed; it can decline if an incumbent is unsuitable. Fortunately the offices are flexible enough to accommodate a variety of incumbents. Able governors have much scope for their talents without opportunities of interfering with governments; incompetent governors can be tolerated without their incompetence doing harm.

The term of office for all eleven governors is five years. They may receive extensions of a few months or a year or two, which is common, or they may receive second terms, which is rare. The advantages of such a turnover in personnel are obvious. Its disadvantage may have a limiting effect. A governor does not have time to become a father-figure, and he may not be able to accumulate a long backlog of experience on which to base Bagehot's rights of encouraging and warning. Being the representative of the Queen does give him instant symbolism, and this is a real advantage to an officer with a short term. But he does not see prime ministers come and go as often as the Queen does. It is more usual in Canada for prime ministers to see governors come and go, a situation which is bound to restrict the average governor's influence. Nevertheless a distinguished governor still has many opportunities for distinguished service, while the limited term is an advantage in cases of weak governors and political appointees.

The person whom the prime minister asks the Queen to appoint as Governor General has been a Canadian since 1952. Before that a variety of Englishmen, Scotsmen, and Irishmen filled the office, some brilliantly, most effectively, some modestly, and none badly. Some, like Lord Tweedsmuir, brought personal distinction to the office, and left their names as part of the tradition of Canada. Some, like Lorne, Connaught, and Athlone, brought prestige at times when Canada needed and wanted it because she had few "front men" of her own. All gave a touch of respectability to Ottawa society when it was trying, with difficulty at first, to develop the spirit and interest of a capital city. In their travels they fostered a non-political national interest away from the capital at a time when Canadians in distant parts had little enough in common.

Meanwhile Canadian life produced available men of distinction, and Canadians, with some initial shy reluctance, began to consider possible candidates of their own. They quarreled over the change, then wondered how it would work, and finally took the chance. Mr. Vincent Massey was the subject of the experiment; everybody watched to see how he would do, and most people agreed he did so well the idea was not bad after all. For General Georges Vanier there was another experiment–the incumbency of a French-speaking Canadian; everybody watched again, and what they saw was magnificent. From then on a Canadian in office was a happy, acceptable practice.

Four Canadian incumbents are scarcely enough to illustrate a trend in the appointing process. They have diplomatic service in common, perhaps, as we have noted, because it has been associated with political independence. Otherwise their qualifications were different. Mr. Massey was a diplomat and business man, and a leader in cultural and educational affairs. He had had a brush with politics, but it was sufficiently unsuccessful and long ago that it could be overlooked. General Vanier was a professional diplomat and soldier with a splendid reputation for integrity. Mr. Roland Michener was so distinguished a Speaker of the House of Commons that he was considered by many members on both sides of the House as a possible permanent Speaker. But he was defeated in an election, whereupon Prime Minister Pearson sent him to India as High Commisioner. The appointment of a Conservative by a Liberal was evidently considered sufficient to nullify political affiliation, and Rideau Hall got what the House of Commons lost. Mr. Jules Léger, at the beginning of his term as this was being written, brought to the office the achievements and experience of a long career as a diplomat and civil servant.

The main difficulty in selecting a Governor General is to find a man who combines the desired qualities and has few disadvantages. He must be distinguished to be respected, and experienced and discreet to understand quickly the demands and limitations of his office. He cannot have a political image, nor can he bear a reputation as a prima donna who is hard to get along with and who might subordinate the office to his personality. Such a combination of attributes and absence of handicaps is rare when a prime minister comes to picking a man. Consequently the possibility of his being a well known, popular, national figure with a sensational reputation is not great, and he will have to make his reputation in office.

This process of appointment is unusual outside the Commonwealth. Many states pick their first citizen by some form of election, or by a kind of political musical chairs in which party potentates allot themselves the top posts. Canadians trust their prime minister to make the choice, and safeguard it only by letting the Queen make the appointment on his advice. This is an example of the prime minister's power being boosted by the existence of the Crown, even to the extent of picking his own constitutional boss. Yet there is no suggestion that the Governor General is therefore the prime minister's puppet, a situation lamentably common elsewhere in countries where election is used. Crown auspices prevent that, and thus enable the two leaders to cooperate from distinct spheres of influence. In some countries where presidents are elected, parties put up candidates, and a prime minister backs one of them and promotes him publicly. The winner may literally owe his success to the political efforts of a prime minister. Even if he does not actually become a puppet, the election may make him appear one, especially when a prime minister forces the choice of candidate on a party, as Mrs. Indira Gandhi did with V.V. Giri in 1969. Furthermore, if the election is open the president often assumes a political image; if it is closed he may assume a party image. And, having to run for office, the candidate often must himself be a politician, or turn himself into one to become well known. If he succeeds too well he may regard himself as a political representative of the people and as such compete with the prime minister.

The Governor General, on the other hand, is a non-political representative of the people selected by their chief political officer, and the prime minister's choice is by comparison not political. Nevertheless, the prime minister does not have a free hand. The position of the Crown and the obvious requirements of

96

the office force his careful consideration and decision. He knows an unwise choice may cause trouble later, especially should His Excellency's personality and experience be inadequate, or should some grave constitutional crisis require the use of emergency powers. Among the weaknesses of the election method is the lack of some person who is directly responsible for relating the man to the job in what can too easily become a popularity contest. It is this responsibility that both ties the Canadian prime minister's hands and justifies this method of selection. There are many instances in other countries where the inadequacy and failures of constitutional presidents have been attributed to what was essentially a popularity contest. Either the man was picked because his popularity overshadowed his lack of qualifications, or because an outstanding alternative candidate did not have enough political contacts to succeed. Furthermore, compromise candidates in such contests are often selected, not because of qualifications, but because abler men had cancelled one another out. In each instance the credibility of the office was lowered. On the other hand, it may also be lowered if the prime minister uses an appointment to bestow a political reward. "To regard the Governor-Generalship as a pension or promotion for a serving local party politician," wrote Prime Minister Robert Menzies of Australia, "seems to me to degrade the conception of the office, to destroy its significance in the public mind and to damage the Crown itself."[6] In discussing the appointment of William McKell, a serving politician, Menzies indicated that it was primarily the members of McKell's own party that "treated him in a casual way, still continuing to regard him as a mere job-holder,"[7] a situation similar to that of Mr. Duplessis' treatment of Mr. Gagnon described earlier.

Selecting a Lieutenant-Governor has not been as definite a process. There have been four kinds of appointees: those with distinguished careers outside of politics; those from outside politics without particularly distinguished careers, but with substantial private means or some special influence, such as being a representative of an interest group; those who had distinguished careers in politics; and those who had average, modest, or unsuccessful careers in politics, or who were defeated candidates, or who were contributors to party funds. These categories are not clear, because it is obviously impossible to classify appointees according to why they were appointed, or to state with certainty whether or not their careers had been distinguished. It is unwise, as we shall note, to ascribe the success or failure of Lieutenant-Governors just to their backgrounds.

But one thing is clear. Regardless of political experience, the Lieutenant-Governor must shed all partisanship while in office. It would be naive to state that none displayed any affinity toward former political colleagues. But the evidence is overwhelming in favor of the high degree of success with which they became and remained politically independent.

If partisanship itself has not been a weakness, an image of partisanship has. The image may be created by a prime minister if he recommends someone who has no obvious claim other than party service, or if there are too many political appointments of any kind. It may also be created by local party stalwarts or interest groups who lobby on behalf of an aspirant, or by an aspirant himself who looks for the position. Even a provincial premier may create a political image, if he is of the same party as the federal government, by using his influence to reward some favorite or get rid of some nuisance.[8] In any event, the public knows as soon as an appointment is made whether or not there is a political image, and its attitude is affected accordingly. Then the new Lieutenant-Governor has to work hard to dispel the image. This task is not difficult if he had a distinguished career in politics, and his ability, service, or integrity were justifications for the appointment. But it is very difficult if he had insufficient personal qualities and experience, because he almost always remains unbelievable.

Another serious criticism of political appointment is its unfairness to politicians themselves. There may be several members of parties not in power in Ottawa who are more experienced and deserving than a successful nominee. To pass them over may deprive the office of excellent incumbents and be a cause of regret to available persons who cannot aspire to the highest post, and to their supporters. Even within the party that is in power in Ottawa, there is no guarantee that the most deserving or suitable person available will be selected. Outstanding lawyers may be considered for judgeships; weaker men may be more *persona grata* than others, especially if they are strongly identified with an interest group; those who have specialized in party leg-work may need encouragement; an opportunity for someone to make a dignified exit from politics may be needed. In such instances the office itself suffers when it is obvious to the public that an appointee has got a "plum" as "his reward".

The backgrounds, assets, and shortcomings of Lieutenant-Governors from Confederation to recent years have been well analyzed by Professor Saywell and others.[9] Many successes of distinguished incumbents and failures of other kinds have been noted by the public. The failures sometimes brought criticism to the office which overshadowed the successes. But there has been a noticeable contribution to the office in recent years through appointments which were not based on political reward and which matched suitably the requirements of the Crown. These appointments included the first woman to become Lieutenant-Governor, Mrs. Pauline McGibbon of Ontario, who was selected in 1974 after a long career of service in many fields, but not in politics.

Reasons for including more non-partisan appointees have been apparent. Many Lieutenant-Governors have so illustrated the value of the office as to set a high standard. A few were either so inadequate as public figures or so indiscreet as to cause official complaint. (I have encountered three recent cases of official complaint, one based on inadequacy and two on indiscretion). The need for political appointments has been diminished by the provision of pensions to politicians. Political appointments may become difficult and unfair when one party is in office in Ottawa for a long time. The drain on the personal resources of incumbents, which discouraged some candidates, has been lessened by the provision of higher salaries and travel expenses by the federal government. And provincial governments have assisted them by providing some allowances, and sharing costs for functions which the government and citizens want performed. Of these reasons, the first two are by far the most important. The Lieutenant-Governor may do so much that it is obviously important and useful to government and citizens that it be done well and with as little purely political identification as possible to limit the field of prospective appointees.

Of all the institutions of government, the governors' offices give the most scope for wives. The wives play major roles in the decorative functions, and perhaps in some of the others too. (No doubt husbands of women Lieutenant-Governors will have the same roles.) Some wives have been more effective than their husbands. When appointments are made, therefore, the qualities of wives are important considerations. If both husband and wife are good at the job the impact of the office is enormous. If one is strong and the other weak the difference is noticeable. If both are weak the Crown's influence may be virtually suspended for five

99

years. No example is more glittering than Mrs. Vanier, who contributed greatly to her husband's successful tenure, and, on his death, was widely suggested as his successor. In all provinces many wives of Lieutenant-Governors have added lustre to the office and usefulness to its functions.

The personalities and qualifications of the governors combine with those of their first ministers in the exercise of many functions of their offices. The governors' consulting roles are among the most important of these functions, and again we note it is the prime minister who is the beneficiary.

We discussed in Chapter Three how a monarch becomes a confidant of a prime minister, particularly if the latter is hard pressed and needs to talk matters over with a non-partisan official he can trust. Much depends on the two people. If each respects the position of the other and they are compatible, the results of their consultations can be unique judgements obtainable nowhere else in government. In most states with this arrangement the two leaders meet regularly each week, and at other times when necessary. This consultation is not, however, joint decision-making. The prime minister normally initiates it, and, whatever passes between them, he alone makes the decisions. The Canadian situation is similar. The governor usually receives copies of important papers, and is kept informed of events and policies. He is consulted by the man who advises him on the use of his powers, and who assumes all responsibility, leaving him none at all.

We must understand how this consultation occurs. A premier will not visit a governor with hat in hand confessing problems and asking guidance. Nor will a sensible governor normally summon a premier and offer advice. A premier with an appreciation of the amenities and of his own need to talk things over will call on a governor regularly, tell him the news informally over coffee and a cigar, and throw some ideas into the conversation in such a way that the governor's opinion is invited. As one ex-premier put it, "I liked to bounce ideas off the governor." The governor will be similarly correct, and give his opinions indirectly to avoid any suggestion of lecturing the premier or telling him what to do. Like two chiefs conducting a pow wow over a peacepipe, they keep their places, maintain their dignity, observe the proprieties, and yet exchange their views.

Should friendship between the two men develop beyond formal relationships, the exchange may be more direct. Nevertheless the premier must still take the initiative, if the consultation is to be effective, by inviting the governor to speak his mind. The governor will then take an attitude such as: "It is not for me to tell you what to do, but, since you have asked me, this is my opinion." They may even argue, with the governor making his points, but always letting the premier win. Almost all successful advice is given this way, and even the most solemn warnings can be so conveyed. This is yet another reason why sensible appointees are needed in these offices. A nonentity whose opinions are of no value can do little with this function; one who obviously received the appointment as a political reward may make little impression on a premier; one who talks party politics with a premier soon loses the latter's confidence; one who takes himself too seriously soon fails, and a premier will not tend to confide in him. A governor with experience, common sense, and tact will give a premier much help because a premier will want to ask for it.

Governors General have had an enormous amount of knowledge and experience. Athlone, for example, knew modern political history from personal experience as few politicians did, and so did Princess Alice, his wife. Tweedsmuir and Alexander understood men and events on a world scale. "The famous Field Marshal's official relations with the Prime Minister and his other advisers were about perfect," writes Mr. St. Laurent's biographer, "combining the utmost circumspection in respecting St. Laurent's leadership of the government with occasional discreet suggestions, and a constant willingness to assist in making the business of running the country a success."[10] For a prime minister to ignore, or deal only formally with, the opportunities this relationship presents is to waste talent, indeed a unique talent that can be consulted or ignored at will and that is non-partisan and confidential. "During nine years of Premiership," said Sir Robert Borden, "I had the opportunity of realizing how helpful may be the advice and counsel of a Governor General in matters of delicacy and difficulty; in no case was consultation with regard to such matters ever withheld; and in many instances I obtained no little advantage and assistance therefrom."[11]

Similar testimony has come from Government House. "I was very fortunate," wrote Mr. Massey about Mr. St. Laurent and Mr. Diefenbaker, "in my personal contacts with both the Prime Ministers who were in office during my time. In both cases we discussed affairs of state privately, informally, and agreeably, with the utmost freedom. . .my advice was often sought and not

101

infrequently offered".[12] Colonel H. Willis-O'Conner, former secretary to the Governor General, has recorded the co-operation between Bessborough and R.B. Bennett. "The Governor General's business experience," he wrote, "and recognized ability in handling of large affairs was of particular assistance to the Prime Minister during the difficult days of the depression. . .an exclusive line was installed to connect Mr. Bennett with the telephone on Lord Bessborough's desk, and to ensure greater privacy, the former always called me first to make certain that the coast was clear. It was all very hush-hush."[13] For reasons already mentioned, such contacts must be hush-hush to be effective, indeed if they are to take place at all.

The personal experience of the three Canadians who have so far completed their terms of office makes an impressive total. And the knowledge they accumulated during their terms was enormous. It seems odd that anyone would expect such advantages to be unused. Mr. Massey told what happened. "I found," he said after he retired, "that the office of the Governor General was very largely misunderstood when I first went to Ottawa. The phrase rubber-stamp was used. It's no rubber stamp. The Governor General's views are solicited by the prime minister frequently and he's encouraged to state them. Decisions are made, of course, by the government, not by him. . .It's a very intimate relationship between two men. . .Each has his function to perform and they meet and discuss matters confidentially whenever it occurs to either of them to do so. . .Another thing about the Governor General, he knows more about what's going on than anybody else by virtue of his office."[14]

This last point is often made about the Queen's knowledge. Politicians and civil servants come and go, while she remains as the only continuing repository of state secrets at high level. Even though the Governor General has a comparatively short term of office, Mr. Massey considered he had the same asset. "People will talk to him, knowing he's completely non-political, as they wouldn't talk to anybody in politics however well they knew them. And also there is a procession of people coming to see him, heads of military bodies and that sort of thing, provincial politicians and so on, over the years. He sees a tremendous number of people and they talk to him with the greatest possible freedom. And so do visiting heads of state. So he's immensely well informed and his opinions are valuable. Not through any virtue of his own but just because of the office he holds."[15] "I learned much," he emphasized, "that no politician could have learned simply by reason of the fact that my post lay outside the realm of controversy."[16]

Mr. Massey's mention of heads of state in this connection suggests a phenomenon I have encountered in many countries. Visiting heads of state, heads of government, and ministers often tend to talk much more freely to the host head of state than to the host head of government. This is particularly true if a visiting head of state wields personal power and has a comparatively weak prime minister; he may prefer to talk frankly only at the top level. Moreover two countries or two governments or two officials are not always politically or personally compatible, and the non-political ear often hears the choicest news and advice for discreet conveyance to the right quarter in the right way.

Wishing to hear Mr. Pearson's opinions, I interviewed him shortly before his death. He confirmed the relationship with enthusiasm. He cited some of his graver crises, and indicated there were times when he could talk over particular vexations with no-one else but the Governor General, with whom he could be frank and from whom he could ask and get sensible, sympathetic advice and encouragement. He too stressed the value of this relationship being non-partisan at the highest level of government. He also emphasized that much depended on the two men. He served with two of his oldest friends, Vanier and Michener, for whom he had the highest respect. Not every prime minister, he said, could enjoy such confidence. And he said that it was the prime minister who had most to gain or lose from the extent of this relationship. Prime Minister Trudeau testified to the gain while he and Mr. Michener were still in office. "I recall," he said, "with personal gratitude the many Wednesday nights since 1968 when you have offered me your encouragement and counsel on the nation's business." "I can testify," he continued, "that you are a man who knows, better than most," where the safe channels are.* Mr. Michener also spoke well of the close relationship.[17]

The consulting role is everywhere a function of the Lieutenant-Governor. But it is not everywhere carried out. Much de-

---

*Speaking at a banquet on Mr. Michener's retirement, Mr. Trudeau told a story of a meeting between the Governor General and a skillful Newfoundland pilot. "I understand," said His Excellency, "That you know where all the rocks are." "Don't know about that, sir," replied the pilot, "but I sure know where all the rocks ain't."[17]

pends on the personalities of the governor and the premier, and there is much variety in the resulting relationships. There are not many accounts, like that about J.J. Bowlen of Alberta, which indicated a cordial relationship[18], or that of Herbert Bruce of Ontario, which revealed both confrontation and harmony[19]. Governors cannot write memoirs about secret matters without damage to the consulting process. But enquiries yield useful, if confidential, revelations of both harmony and discord behind the scenes.

A distinguished, experienced, and discreet Lieutenant-Governor almost always enjoys the results described by Mr. Massey and Mr. Pearson. Like John B. MacNair, who was in effect "Mr. New Brunswick" because of his spectacular career as Premier, Chief Justice, and Lieutenant Governor, and Grant MacEwan, who could be similarly identified with Alberta because of his scholarship and writings on western Canada, such men display all the value of the Crown. A distinguished, experienced, but indiscreet governor, on the other hand, has an uncomfortable relationship with the average premier; with a powerful premier he has intermittent quarrels or he is ignored. A Lieutenant-Governor of average qualities enjoys an average consulting relationship with a premier who is in office a few years, and sometimes very little with a long-time premier. A nonentity must be content with only the formalities.

As for the premiers, they act on their own inclinations as well as on His Honour's attributes. Some tend to resent their second place in the governmental hierarchy; some are diligent in observing it. Some consult the Lieutenant-Governor regularly; others tell him as little as possible, although they usually find it expedient to keep him informed at times of crisis. On the whole the relationships have been overwhelmingly cordial. This situation has been remarkable because premiers, especially in seven of the ten provinces, are pretty powerful potentates in relation to what they do, and the temptation to present themselves as the image of their provinces as well as of their governments is strong. But yielding to this temptation does not pay in the Canadian constitutional system. Hepburn and Duplessis, who did yield and openly denigrated a governor, soon tried to present such an image and failed. Embarrassed and chagrined fellow citizens smashed, not only the provincial image they presented, but their personal image as well. And, because they and their supporters depended too much on their images, their parties soon entered the political wilderness after their deaths.

104

The few difficulties between governors and premiers that became public knowledge illustrated why the Crown should not be involved in political disputes. Governors General and Lieutenant-Governors, like the Queen, "can do no wrong" because governments must take responsibility for what they do. A premier who lets a governor be a centre of controversy is himself violating the constitution by not taking responsibility and by shifting the blame to where it does not belong. In view of the Lieutenant-Governor's role in provincial sovereignty, for example, the use of his office in Quebec by some critics as a target for opposing the "federal presence" is neither fair to him nor in the interest of the Quebec government. Quebec premiers are no different from those in other provinces. Mitchell Hepburn used the Lieutenant-Governor's office for political advantage when he criticized Government House in an election in what Lieutenant-Governor Herbert Bruce called one of "the most irresponsible types of appeals to passion." Although friendly with Bruce, Hepburn carried out his threat of closing the house during his feud with Prime Minister King after using the issue to persuade King to appoint one of his defeated ministers to the Senate.[20] In Newfoundland bitter feelings arose when Lieutenant-Governor Campbell MacPherson was evidently not given sufficient notice of the appointment of his successor, Fabian O'Dea, and, according to Premier Smallwood, "Diefenbaker just told MacPherson to get out. He threw him out." The premier's subsequent relations with O'Dea were naturally strained by the relations between the premier and the prime minister.[21] In all such issues observers tend to examine the governor's role, and find out later that it was a premier who deserved the scrutiny, especially when he could talk and the governor could not.

Once in a while a Lieutenant-Governor causes difficulties. He may take himself too seriously, attempt to interfere in governmental matters, or scold a premier for doing something he does not like. The governor may be right, but unable to participate in the right way. Or he may be wrong, and persist in following an inept course of action. Perhaps his wife may provoke trouble, as Mrs. C.A. Banks of British Columbia did on the famous occasion in 1948 when she scolded some wives of M.L.A.'s who were late for a Government House luncheon, and the matter was raised in the legislature. In all instances it is the premier's right to advise the governor, perhaps even to tell him to mind his own business, or ask him to restrain his wife. This is almost always as far as such difficulties go. Should more persistent vexations arise, the governor should consult the federal government. If he does not, the premier may do it. This move is effective; it is a quiet but firm approach which a mistaken governor must heed because he cannot incur the displeasure of two governments. As we shall note, consultation with Ottawa is now necessary in connection with the governor's use of emergency powers. In lesser matters, the premier, a federal cabinet minister from the province concerned, perhaps the prime minister, may inform or restrain a governor with a discreet suggestion or firm advice. Indeed there is now little scope for a governor to do much harm because he is the most advised official in the government.

There is no evidence that a Lieutenant-Governor's success depends on whether or not he is an ex-politician. Men with no experience as politicians, but who have been prominent in other fields, often have a better grasp of the possibilities of the job because they are not tempted to be political, and because they may know more about provincial affairs and public opinion than many politicians. If they match or exceed the premier in personal prestige, they often enjoy his confidence because they can give him advice that he might not take from another politician. Indeed it is not difficult to notice that the majority of Lieutenant-Governors have had far more experience than the majority of ministers. Governors in this category also enjoy the respect of the public, men like Frank Ross of British Columbia and Sir Leonard Outerbridge of Newfoundland.

As for ex-politicians, one rule holds with few exceptions. The more successful they were in political office the more successful they were as Lieutenant-Governors of this category, the less inclined they were to meddle, and the closer their relations were with the premiers. The weakest Lieutenant-Governors, again with few exceptions, have been minor politicians or defeated candidates whom no-one could take seriously, who were too eager to make in office the reputations denied them in political or professional life, and failed because they could not carry it off. The fact that authorities discuss such people only in confidence is perhaps for them a merciful oblivion.

There is far more to the offices of Governor General and Lieutenant-Governor than the personalities of the incumbents because, in Ernest Lapointe's words, it can be said of each one: "he represents law; he represents order; he represents authority."[22]

106

SIX

INFLUENCES ON EXECUTIVE POWERS

HAVING THE GOVERNORS as part of the executive facilitates practice in government and reinforces responsibility. Because certain powers are not actually given to the governments,
their retention by the governors encourages caution in their use
by the governments. Indeed several useful powers are thereby labelled "to be used sparingly, if at all". These, it must be emphasized, are not emergency powers of the governors, but special
practical powers lent to the governments, but not given to them.

A veto power over provincial legislation placed directly in the
hands of a federal government is difficult to arrange and tolerate.
We have therefore developed a complicated ritual which permits
a veto, but also discourages much use of it. Sections 56 and 90 of
the British North America Act provide that the Governor General-in-Council may disallow a provincial act within one year of
its reaching Ottawa. Sections 55 and 90 enable the Lieutenant-
Governor to reserve the Governor General's assent from a provincial bill, and the bill does not become law unless the Governor

General gives his assent within a year of receiving it.* There were, according to Dr. Forsey, 112 cases of disallowance up to 1943, and 70 cases of reservation up to 1961. The power of disallowance seems now to be in a state of suspension. Practice and federal pronouncements have made it clear that Lieutenant-Governors should reserve only on instructions from Ottawa. When, for example, Lieutenant-Governor Frank L. Bastedo of Saskatchewan reserved a bill in 1961, Prime Minister Diefenbaker advised the Governor General to give his assent, and made it clear in the House of Commons that His Honour should have consulted federal authorities before acting.[1] Indeed Mr. Diefenbaker, as we shall see, had already advised the Lieutenant-Governor of Newfoundland two years earlier to delay assent to a bill until the federal goverment had considered it.

Whether or not these powers are operable as far as the governors are concerned has often been debated. But two things are clear. First, the powers exist, and, even if governors do not use them on their own initiative, they can threaten consultation with Ottawa in unusual situations, and governments can advise governors to use them. Second, occasions may arise when federal governments want, and should have, some emergency control over provincial legislation of a particularly offensive nature. No-one would want to use the powers of disallowance and reservation under even the most extraordinary circumstances; but their existence may be a deterrent to provincial governments, and it does enable federal governments to threaten their use. And it also enables aggrieved citizens to demand their use as a tactic in a confrontation with a government.

The famous Aberhart legislation has often been discussed in this connection. Actually, the threat of disallowance is more sub-

---

*The Lieutenant-Governor assents to acts of the provincial legislature on behalf of the Governor General. Copies then go to Ottawa. On a rare occasion some very serious objection to an act may prompt a Lieutenant-Governor to reserve the assent after consultation with Ottawa or after instructions from Ottawa to do it, and the act then becomes law if the Governor General-in-Council (the Governor General and cabinet) give the assent. After the Lieutenant-Governor has given assent the Governor General-in-Council can disallow the act (the chances of his doing it are not great) within one year of its receipt. The appropriate channel of communication in these matters is from the Lieutenant-Governor to the Department of the Secretary of State.

tle. Premier J. Walter Jones of Prince Edward Island had a dispute with the Packinghouse Workers Union, and he settled a strike at Canada Packers by taking over the plant. He told me himself that Finance Minister J.L. Ilsley, following pressure by the union on the federal government, had paid him a quiet visit and threatened disallowance of the province's labour legislation of 1948 unless he undertook to change the act at the next session. He did. In 1959 the Canadian Labour Congress asked the federal government for reservation, or, failing that, disallowance of Premier J.R. Smallwood's legislation designed to end a loggers' strike that became a national sensation. Prime Minister Diefenbaker confidentially asked the Lieutenant-Governor of Newfoundland to delay assent until the legislation was studied in Ottawa, but Lieutenant-Governor Campbell MacPherson nevertheless gave immediate assent.[2] There have been other such threats. These issues do not clarify the use of these powers. It is no doubt useful not to clarify them, because, if they were too clearly defined, governors and politicians might be tempted to use them more. They indicate in practice a handy ghost which, if not actually made to materialize, can be invoked in an official hex on someone who may need it. And the unions' demands in the instances cited indicated an effective vehicle for public intervention. All this is practical, because, while citizens in their federal capacities might agree to a clearer veto power, in their provincial capacities they would prefer instead the possible resurrection of an old ghost.

Another power of the government increased and controlled by a governor's store of powers concerns the dismissal of ministers. Part V of his letters-patent enables the Governor General "to remove from his office, or to suspend from the exercise of the same, any person exercising any office within Canada" under the name or authority of the Queen. The Lieutenant-Governor has a similar power within his province. We will discuss later the dismissal of the whole cabinet. But here we should consider the dismissal of individual ministers, a problem so well provided for under the Crown that Canadians do not know it exists.

This matter is one of the most difficult in contemporary government, and the need for some kind of arrangement is well illustrated throughout the world. Summary dismissal, public humiliation, imprisonment, even "liquidation", are now commonplace in numerous republics, despite their parliaments and what their laws may provide. And many politicians survive removal only by going into hiding or exile. Aside from the feelings and safety of victims, who were serving their country and people in their ways, the effect on governing is great. Humiliation, whether real or fancied, deserved or undeserved, lingers, rankles, and may become the force behind many plots and disruptions of public business in the interest of revenge. It is government itself that suffers, and the citizens who pay the cost. And it is the citizens who get the impression, alas! so often justified, that politics is "dirty", that politicians are not to be trusted, and that their interests are being sacrificed. Any action that assuages this difficulty is a practical contribution to public life in any system, especially in democracy which places so much stress on the dignity of individuals and the importance of government service.

In Canada and countries with similar arrangements politicians lead a charmed life by comparison. For them dismissal has presented no personal danger or public humiliation, a fact they and citizens take for granted. The action is so simple—a short diversion of a potent power through a well insulated container to make it more tolerable.

The advantage of the Canadian arrangement is the fact that dismissal by the Crown on the advice of the prime minister is more effective, and yet more controlled, than dismissal by the prime minister direct.

A governor may dismiss a minister if such rare and drastic action becomes necessary; and he and everyone else know that he must take the advice of the prime minister. In fact, however, such a dismissal would be almost inconceivable in Canada. A minister in trouble would resign at the prime minister's request rather than incur the supreme indignity of dismissal by the Crown, and many ministers have departed from governments in this way. In practice, a minister may not want to depart; indeed he may have a reasonable grievance and consider his removal unfair. He may even have to go because of some difficulty for which the whole cabinet was responsible and his sacrifice became necessary to save the government. Should he prove stubborn any one of four things may happen. He may refuse to go and be dismissed; he may refuse, but be persuaded to resign; he may be "bought off" with some other appointment to assuage his frustration; or the prime minister may give in and let him stay. A fifth alternative is a reluctance on the part of the prime minister to initiate matters at all, however much he would like to remove the colleague. If the first of these alternatives is unlikely, the others are all common.*

Incidents like these rarely become public knowledge, and it is only when one hears details that one realizes how common they are. Canadians may suspect the problem if they ask themselves why even Mr. King, who was competent at wielding the big stick, found it necessary to ask for some resignations in advance and keep them for possible need, rather than wait for the need and then ask. In the cases of which I have been told in Canada and elsewhere, the action was subtle. A stubborn minister who says "I will not resign, dismiss me if you dare" will not get a letter of dismissal. Colleagues may be able to convince him. Usually they will not try. If all else fails he may be invited to the official residence for a friendly chat, be told that no-one wants to dismiss him, and gently and with dignity be persuaded to resign. The tactic involves cooling his reason and making him see his duty, something a prime minister may be unable to do in the heat of the quarrel. The need for the tactic often arises from the fact that the most blameworthy ministers usually raise the most fuss and have to be prevented from embarrassing the government, perhaps undermining it altogether. I knew a stubborn Canadian minister who was justly removed in this way with much-needed help from the Lieutenant-Governor; the minister never spoke to the premier again. Such situations often arise in coalition governments. There are occasions when a prime minister needs all the help possible in such difficult circumstances. And it is not normal for him to receive this help from his cabinet colleagues, however much they may approve his action.

This kind of dismissal power also provides a hindrance to the prime minister's use of it. The prime minister may be wrong, even unjust, perhaps jealous. Disposing of heirs-apparent who become too popular is an old tactic. And some prime ministers cannot forgive colleagues who oppose them in cabinet. Other ministers can sometimes protect a minister who is threatened with a forced resignation; more often they cannot. R. MacGregor Dawson's dramatic description of the conscription crisis of 1944, in which cabinet ministers of the highest ability and integrity saw J.L. Ralston dismissed from Mackenzie King's cabinet, illustrates

---

*The Hon. Judy LaMarsh has described Prime Minister Pearson's difficulties in securing the resignations of some of his ministers.[3]

the feelings in such cases. "Disturbed by a sense of guilt that they had allowed themselves to be the compliant accessories of a ruthless coup, and smarting with resentment against the Prime Minister. . .they looked upon the dismissal as an act of unforgivable callousness. . .Meanwhile they found some comfort in private recriminations against the greater guilt of the man whose hands had raised the pole-axe on high and brought it down on the head of their brother."[4] But Dawson was writing about distinguished men in a genuine crisis. Ministers of lesser calibre in ordinary circumstances allow such removals to take place with fewer pangs of conscience. At least that is all that happens; many contemporary ministers elsewhere have gone to jail or been banished for less than Colonel Ralston's support of conscription.

Governors will not get involved in the merits of dismissals. It is not their business, and it is the prime minister's responsibility. But the influence of good governors is present in the drama in discouraging outright dismissal, perhaps only in smoothing ruffled feathers. Two facts are important. It is much easier for a prime minister (or anyone else) to say "you're fired" when he does it directly than it is to say "I am recommending your dismissal to the governor" (or, in the case of others, to a board). This difference is a hurdle. The second fact is the matter of explaining the situation to a governor, even though the governor must take the advice. If there are doubts about the dismissal, or if the minister is being treated unfairly, it will be a difficult explanation to make to a distinguished governor, and a prime minister may well hesitate. Even the hardest-hearted pole-axe wielder would have found it difficult to make such an explanation to Governor General Vanier and bear the look he would be sure to get from that saintly man. As far as smoothing ruffled feathers is concerned, two things may happen. A governor, in accepting advice, may show his distaste, something he has every right to do, and ask the prime minister to let his colleague down more easily and save his dignity. He may be of more direct help, by privately expressing appreciation for past service without taking a personal stand on the contemporary problem, a tactic that is far more effective and deserving than the cold letter which a prime minister will send his victim.

An example in Canada's smallest province illustrates how far a premier may go; and it is not unlike the Nehru-Radhakrishnan issue already cited. Premier John H. Bell of Prince Edward Island advised Lieutenant-Governor Murdoch MacKinnon in 1924 to dismiss Attorney-General J.J. Johnston for allegedly advocating in Ottawa without local permission the addition by the federal government of an extra judge to the provincial supreme court. A minute of censure against the minister had even appeared in the minutes of the executive council. Such an extraordinary occurrence roused the suspicion of the Lieutenant-Governor who, upon investigating, found no such minute had been passed. He refused to dismiss the minister or sign the minutes of council, whereupon the premier repeated his advice to do so. Meanwhile the whole cabinet heard of the bogus minute because the governor had asked questions. In what must have been a dramatic confrontation, the cabinet members together interrupted the meeting between the Lieutenant-Governor and the premier, learned what was going on, and insisted that the premier erase the minute which they had never passed and withdraw his advice to the Lieutenant-Governor.[5]

I have heard incidents like this described many times in Canada and elsewhere, and three features of them have struck me, particularly after interviewing ministers who elsewhere have been abruptly dismissed, banished, or put in jail. One is the value of letting the prime minister use a power he does not actually possess. The whole approach to that power by him and others is different; and the power itself is taken more responsibly and seriously. Another is the manner in which a wise governor can soften the callousness of a premier or cushion the effects of it, as well as make deserved dismissal more acceptable. The third feature is the way all this leaves a victim of politics with the feeling that he could endure the action of a government or party if the state itself through its head seems to treat him with kindness and gratitude.

Another purpose of the governors' powers which helps government is to strengthen institutions established by parliament and appointments made by the government. Part IV of the Governor General's letters-patent "authorize and empower Our Governor General to constitute and appoint, in Our name and on Our behalf all such Judges, Commissioners, Justices of the Peace, and other necessary Officers (including diplomatic and consular officers) and Ministers of Canada, as may be lawfully constituted or appointed by Us." The Lieutenant-Governor makes similar appointments under the Crown that are within provincial jurisdiction. These powers, exercised on the advice of the Cabinet and countersigned by a responsible official, may seem to be only relics

113

of by-gone days when governors wielded power directly. But they are not. They are valuable reinforcements for executive authority and protections for the appointees, the existence or absence of which are major factors in government in Canada and in every country around the world.

There is in practice an enormous difference between an appointment by a state and an appointment by a government. Even though a government recommends an appointment by a state, it can rarely confer sufficiently strong auspices on behalf of a state, parliament, or people. Whole governments change with democratic processes, coups d'état, or constitutional crises. They can be popular, disliked, or feared, perhaps even be regarded with ridicule or contempt. Within one government ministers come and go; what they do may last, or end with their departure; their reputations may shine brilliantly or may be tarnished by mistakes or scandal; they may be mediocrities or incompetents with no reputations at all. Meanwhile parliaments are necessarily transitory; and public opinion changes with political fashion.

Nevertheless, certain functions must be performed over a period of time for the whole state, or must be carried out without suggestion either of political auspices or of the pressure of passing fads. These are the functions that must remain and operate over and above the interests of a government of the day, to continue from administration to administration, and to serve, not just the "ins", but also the "outs". If the official stamp of approval on such a function is too closely identified with the government that recommends it or the fashion that prompts it, it may later be rendered ineffective by the subsequent unpopularity of that government or the suspicion of a new government; or it might be ignored during the rise of another temporary fashion. Politicians will rarely admit it, but new governments, whether of the same political persuasion as the old or not, tend to be suspicious of, or impatient with, the projects, policies, and personnel of the old. The state, its institutions, its policies, and its permanent servants require protection against such unstable auspices. So do the citizens whose business is being done and who pay the cost.

These unstable and costly auspices are everywhere noticed in countries where changing regimes are able to confer only their own temporary identity on institutions and appointees. In Canada, on the other hand, a government is able to make its appointees more effective by conferring on them the official sanctity

114

of the state that the government itself as a democratic body is rightly unable to bestow. Mr. St. Laurent could choose a judge, but the judge immediately lost his identity with the patron and the government, and became Her Majesty's justice, a status that carried him protected into the Diefenbaker term.* Mr. Diefenbaker's administration could select an officer to be a general whereupon the latter got a commission from the Governor General which the Pearson government had to recognize. By contrast, the impact of changing governmental auspices was obvious while the Canadian Bill of Rights bore the popular title "Diefenbaker Bill of Rights"; even though it had been passed by parliament, the resulting controversy impeded its acceptability until the Drybones case gave it judicial auspices and compelled more governmental and public respect.** Indeed prime ministers and their ministers are themselves assured of a continuing respectability through the vicissitudes of politics by membership in Her Majesty's Privy Council for Canada. The practicality of even this formal recognition may be appreciated when one compares it with situations in many republics where governments suffer from lack of respectable experienced elder statesmen with status, or where retired politicians must live in obscurity, go into hiding, or flee the country when new politicians take over.

Institutions also illustrate a need for higher auspices. We have noted the opposition's status. The term "royal commission" denotes superior methods of appointment; nation-wide or province-wide recognition on a continuing basis, and absence of political interference; careful investigation; and impeccable procedure, that no other committee of enquiry except a court can command. If John Doe gets into trouble with the law his rights and the interest of the citizenry are made clearer by calling his case "Doe vs. The Queen" and his accuser a "crown prosecuter" than by any suggestion of Doe vs. the government. "Crown land" implies a greater degree of public ownership than "government property". Even such devoted socialists as Clement Attlee and

---

*Canadians would not refer, for example, to the "St. Laurent Court" like Americans did, and still do, to the "Roosevelt Court".

**This case alleged discrimination against Indians in penalties in the Indian Act for infractions of liquor regulations. It became a legal milestone when the Supreme Court of Canada invoked the Canadian Bill of Rights against the discrimination.

Herbert Morrison, who first organized the "crown corporations" which Canada later copied, were insistent on the removal of all identity of such bodies with the government of the day, its politics, and its civil servants.

Symbols also illustrate this identification. As we have noted, photographs of heads of state are evident throughout most countries, on office walls, postage stamps, currency, often on posters in the streets. Crowns, hammer and sickle, crosses, and other designs are in common use to identify states and political systems on flags, stationery, decorations, and the like. From the standpoint of the state, the effectiveness of national symbols depends greatly on the extent to which they are identified with the state itself, rather than with a regime, a temporary jurisdiction, government, even with just an administrative process. When, in Canada, the crown, coat of arms, or picture of the sovereign are used by the governors in performing their duties, and by parliament to mark special functions, the identification is much broader and longer lasting because they reflect the whole government, culture, and tradition. The effects are noticeable in the difference between attitudes toward "Royal Mail" and "Canada Post", comparison between the state's auspices implied in "Queen's Printer" and the government's interest in "Information Canada". As for impact, state symbols tend to retain it when they are identified in a limited way with the non-political summit of government. They lose it to the point where they are scarcely appreciated anymore, when they become commonplace on souvenirs, routine stationery, sweatshirts, and travellers' knapsacks; when they are used continually by government to identify and reinforce itself; or when they are desecrated in attempts to oppose or remove a government.*

The significance of strengthening appointments and institutions in Canada is also revealed when there are no crown auspices and much identification with the government. Patronage then becomes the dominant image as the people suspect partisan "fav-

---

*The danger of identifying symbols with government rather than with the state was illustrated when the Canadian Federation of Civil Liberties and Human Rights Associations suggested that a bill to prevent desecration of the maple leaf flag "constitutes a danger to freedom of speech. . .It will be used primarily against protestors who use the flag to symbolize their opposition to policies of the government, as has occurred recently in the United States."[6]

116

ours", "hand-outs", and "rewards".* The opposition may make careful note of this, so that when it comes to power it may replace one patronage list with another. The difference in auspices may become even more noticeable when a government becomes careless in making crown appointments and identifies them too much with its own interests. The prevalence of petty party patronage in the appointment of Queen's Counsel, for example, may be convenient to governments and parties, but it destroys the credibility of the appointees. "Debase" was the word used when even the Manitoba Bar recommended the abolition of the appointments on the ground that they "have become political with no regard given to merit or to any other qualifications."[7] The same criticism arises when governments attempt to bestow honours or are careless in recommending them. An institution that suffers from this carelessness cannot remove the political stigma from itself, even though the public blames it for having it. Careless appointments on the part of governments reduce the credibility and effectiveness of the Senate, despite all the hard work and practical influence of abler members of it. And the Crown itself suffers when a government selects an obviously partisan appointee to a lieutenant-governorship when other, and much more deserving, candidates are available.

A governor's auspices may reinforce other governmental actions in the same way they do the appointing procedure. External relations with other governments present an obvious example. An action labelled "Governor General-in-Council" or "Lieutenant-Governor-in-Council" carries more weight and invites less contemporary criticism and future aggravation than a mere cabi-

---

*Interesting aspects of state patronage are illustrated by one practice followed in several countries. Some might consider that "By Appointment, Grocers, to Her Majesty the Queen" is an anachronistic, perhaps undemocratic, title for a food store. Aside from the quality and service which the award recognizes and encourages, it is more useful to the public than the costly and undemocratic patronage which governments give to firms in return for political favours. Patronage, inevitable in government, is more sensible if it is conferred openly; and crown auspices are an effective instrument for doing openly and without expense what otherwise is more costly, perhaps harmful, behind the scenes. Which is the more democratic: "By Appointment, Suppliers of Whiskey" because of quality and without obligation, or leading supplier of whiskey to a provincial liquor store because of substantial contributions to the political party in power?

net declaration. Even the auspices of legislatures may be inadequate, however supreme they may be in their jurisdictions, either when one is weakened by too many quarrelling parties, or when another is dominated by a huge majority or an autocratic premier. It is a subsequent government or legislature, resenting its predecessor's auspices, that will denigrate an earlier action that identifies the state or province with the predecessors, and will make every effort to change the image.

It is in foreign affairs that this matter is most obvious. As we noted earlier, a government's image may be inadequate in presenting a country's interests abroad. Sometimes the less said elsewhere about a government or its leader the better. The government and leader will never admit this, however, and often they undermine with their image every international action they take. They might be more successful if they act in the name of some higher authority which, though it does not itself initiate action, presents a more acceptable image of the country itself. The state visit is often used for this purpose. It is not difficult for other governments to deal with Canada, either "on principle" or in practice, because the Crown represents the people, whatever the popularity or political persuasion of the government, and despite differences which governments do have from time to time with other governments. Pablo Cassals swore never to return to Spain while Franco was alive; it would be highly unlikely for a Canadian to so identify his country or province with either a government or its leader. Canada has governments, not regimes; the Crown ensures recognition of the difference; and the governments are the beneficiaries.

The granting of pardons further illustrates the value of identification with the Crown. Pardons are granted by governors on the advice of governments. Pardon allowed by a government and given in its name is not as effective as one recommended by a government and given by a governor. The first process is too easily regarded as just a "letting him out" by an administration; the second is a final act of clemency and forgiveness by a state. A government could not put back in jail a man pardoned by its predecessor for the same offence; and it could only release a man for good reason. But it is obvious in many republics that, despite laws, governments let people out of jail later to put them back in, associate pardons with political recanting, or link clemency with changes of administrations, perhaps just of leaders. Even a supreme law or written constitution may be ineffective in determining the power of pardon in places where it is identified with a regime, and not associated with a non-political institution that acts as a custodian of the power and the rights of the pardoned.

A final reinforcement of the executive must be noted. Because of crown auspices, everyone knows the status of government and recognizes its legitimacy, a situation not too common in some republics. Even where a government bears a popular mandate and seems to have the support of a legislature, its own image, titles, policies and achievements are often not enough to give it sufficiently powerful auspices as the rightful executive. Canadians, on the other hand, can be certain that a prime minister, absent on a visit, will not be replaced, that other governments will recognize any Canadian governments, and that usurpation is most unlikely. "It's all right for some of you chaps," a Commonwealth prime minister had to say to some colleagues at the Ottawa Commonwealth Conference of 1973, "you've got armies at home to keep an eye on things for you".[8] Even the army may be unreliable, as two republican presidents in the Commonwealth, Mujibur Rahman of Bangladesh and General Gowan of Nigeria, found in 1975 when the first was murdered, and the second was replaced while absent at a conference. In Canada the army is not needed for the stability of executive power. Politicians can deal with it themselves, not on the basis of any alleged virtues which they may possess and easily lose, but on the auspices of the Crown which give them a formal respectability that reinforces legitimacy. And this respectability is particularly needed by politicians as a defence against other politicians who in the heat of political battle may undermine legitimacy if they can. To citizens, the impact of higher auspices in government should come as no surprise since they everywhere invoke similar auspices in religion, commerce and personal life by means of patronage, testimony, and sponsorship.

The auspices of the Crown and the identification of government with it facilitate teamwork within the government. All Canada's servants in executive, legislative, judicial, and administrative branches work under the Crown as a formal but practical official umbrella which permits both separate and associated identities that are not found in many republics. "The problem of a satisfactory identification and distinction of the management element is most difficult to solve," wrote the eminent Canadian authority A.D.P. Heeney. "The ancient, and honourable, concept of the Queen and her servants is no longer a sufficient or accurate description of a relationship which has changed greatly since the last century. Nevertheless, one of the great strengths of the public service continues to be the traditional sense of common cause and common responsibility which binds together those who have undertaken to serve the state and its citizens."[9]

These examples of governors' powers enabling the executive to do things which might otherwise be difficult reflect a prevailing healthy attitude of citizens toward their government. Citizens must have a government, but they will only go so far for so long in supporting and respecting it if the facade of power which is presented to them is too garish, and if the actions of government are too blatant. They suspect, often correctly, that such a government is more concerned with its power than their business. Nevertheless they want colour in their system and evidence that things are happening. If the citizens are to retain control over the government there must be a balance between these two facts. A lack of balance has been evident in many countries where governments possess and wield too much power directly and are too obvious in doing it, and where governmental image-making takes too much of their time and the people's money. Either such a government is thrown out by jealous rivals and impatient citizens, or it consolidates its position by purging rivals and cutting the freedom of citizens.

In Canada, on the other hand, governments are powerful and citizens are free. The facade of executive power presents an intricate mosaic rather than a striking pattern, and the resulting actions are indirect and restrained. The great powers of premiers are disguised and are therefore tolerable. Because premiers are constitutional *éminences grises* they can be political *éminences brillantes*, of whom a public does not quickly get jealous, and to whom citizens can give more power if they can slip it to them discreetly through the governors rather than hand it to them directly. The governors take on the constitutional *brillant* and the powers, but nobody fears or gets jealous of them because everyone knows they must let the ministers control the powers. An excellent example is the power to dissolve parliament. Republics are reluctant to bestow this power on a head of government. In Canada we give this power to the governor to exercise on the prime minister's advice. In fact, as we shall see, the prime minister determines when dissolution is to take place, except perhaps

120

in the gravest of emergencies, and there are good reasons why he should do so. This arrangement is easy for citizens to tolerate. It would likely be impossible to actually give the power to the prime minister in a written constitution; that would be too obvious and too direct.

All this ritual that surrounds the exercise of political power is perfectly natural. Man's other major powers are handled in the same way. He makes love with wooing, worships with formalities, eats with customs, entertains with observances, does business with procedures, and dies with rites. What makes him do it is often incomprehensible. But he seems to know, as do other animals, that direct approaches are unreliable, and often intolerable. There is no reason why public business should be an exception. Many governments and men in them have failed, despite perhaps the best intentions, because they took direct approaches that simply did not work. And many others have been successful. The reason usually is inexplicable except in terms of natural actions in the face of human instincts. The governors do not operate by means of direct approaches; they rely on indirect actions, developed by the Crown, that are shown to work in government. Wooing, formalities, customs, observances, procedures, and rites are therefore natural reinforcements and compensations provided by the Crown in the governing of Canada and its provinces.

SEVEN

EMERGENCY POWERS

THE OFFICES of Governor General and Lieutenant-Governor are constitutional fire extinguishers with a potent mixture of powers for use in great emergencies. Like real extinguishers, they appear in bright colours and are strategically located. But everyone hopes their emergency powers will never be used; the fact they are not used does not render them useless; and it is generally understood there are severe penalties for tampering with them.

The emergency powers of the Crown have developed because serious trouble is inevitable in government, and some special apparatus must be kept in reserve ready for use should other safety devices fail. The trouble must be serious. To use the Crown's powers on ordinary troubles would make a mess, and weaken their potential force in a real crisis.

Remedies for ordinary troubles are well known in Canada. Parliament and cabinet can remove each other to seek a fresh popular mandate. The courts can judge if legislation is beyond the competence of those that make it. The powers of public servants and organizations are set forth, usually with remedies for misuse. Special safety devices are included within institutions, such as solidarity and secrecy in cabinets, provisions for expressing want of confidence in legislatures, and disciplinary and dismissal procedures in other places. And the press and public can declare both confidence in and opposition to any section of the government. All this apparatus is used for the common problems of government, and it can also cope effectively with most thundering rows of serious proportions. The emergency powers of the Crown can therefore be left undisturbed, except for the periodic attentions of lawyers and professors who dust them off now and then, examine their capacity, and tell everyone when and how they can be used. Once in a while somebody suggests they should be discarded; but then a politician commits an extraordinary depredation and reinforces the need for them.

If the emergency powers are not used, their existence is, nevertheless, a deterrent to overheated government. Just as a painter will be cautious in using a blowtorch near an automatic sprinkler, a prime minister will at times of great temptation be careful how near he goes to setting off the supreme constitutional device. We do not need reminders of how far heads of government do go in contemporary affairs, and how easily they can hoodwink the people into thinking the most tragic extremes of action are for the public good. In Canada, it is not difficult to think of politicians who, if unrestrained, would take the ultimate step in a fearful gamble, if they were able to do it. Nor is it difficult to think of occasions when it is desirable that a governor remind a premier that an outrageous executive action is beyond a premier's constitutional mandate, and that emergency powers exist.

Could Canada have problems of such serious dimensions that the ordinary apparatus and public opinion could not cope with them and the Crown's powers would have to be used? The answer must be a clear and unmistakable "Yes". In this age when we like to think we are sophisticated about out public affairs, governments and constitutions are failing and falling with embarrassing regularity. They had emergency apparatus, but most did not have a sufficiently powerful constitutional instrument to cope with a major conflagration. Aside from the resulting political upheavals, the cost in both money and lives is astronomical. There is no evidence that Canada can safely claim political immunity.

At what point in a crisis does the use of the emergency powers of the Crown become justified in a democratic parliamentary system? This point is reached when normal controls cannot operate, and the crisis gets out of hand, and certain officials take advantage of the crisis to act unconstitutionally in their own interests. It may also be reached when officials try to circumvent normal controls by acting secretly behind the scenes, and by preventing retribution from those who exercise normal controls, and from the public. It is at this point that the Governor General and Lieutenant-Governor may invoke emergency powers. But they face a powerful deterrent–they must be sure they have reached the danger point, and that their actions will stand up to the subsequent judgement of other institutions and the people. Otherwise a prime minister can cry "false alarm", and the governor will take the blame and perhaps even be forced to resign.

An important emergency power is the selection of a government when there is a crisis. A governor always selects a government; indeed it is his invitation that gives legal sanction to it. But he must call on the person who has the support of a majority in parliament to form a government, and accept the prime minister's nominees as ministers. This choice is obvious when the people and a parliament can make it obvious after an election, or when a prime minister announces his retirement sufficiently in advance to enable his party to have a leadership convention. Normally, therefore, a governor has no discretion because his decision is made for him. Where the power becomes an emergency power is in circumstances where the people and a parliament cannot make a decision, a stalemate arises, and a governor is given no name on whom to call.

If such a crisis takes place, a governor does not pick someone to form a government. The emergency power enables him to intervene in the picking only by encouraging and helping others to do the picking themselves. The resulting nominee does not need his confidence, but the confidence of parliament. The governor does not sustain him in office afterwards; parliament does. The reasons for this intervention have already been described. In theory parliament makes the choice; in practice it may need help from a non-partisan source in dealing with the peculiarities of human nature. The people need a government in crisis that has a stable constitution mandate. Should this need arise in Canada, the governors are equipped to meet it.

The vacuum left by the death of a prime minister or a premier in office may cause a particularly difficult emergency. Should party indecision or a scramble for power follow the demise of a powerful leader, governments often suffer a period of turmoil, and the party in power sometimes disintegrates. There has not been such an event in the federal government since Sir John Thompson died in 1894, but the deaths in quick succession of Premier Duplessis in September, 1959 and Premier Sauvé in January, 1960 highlighted the problem. Mr. Sauvé's name was presented to Lieutenant-Governor Onésime Gagnon in a petition signed by the ministers who had served under Duplessis, and His Honor accepted it. The choice was obvious enough. But when Sauvé died the choice was not obvious, and the Lieutenant-Governor called on Antonio Barrette after his name had been approved at a meeting of ministers and ratified by a Union Nationale caucus. What happened during these meetings and afterwards indicates the value of a governor's participation during an emergency.[1]

The issue illustrated the duty of a governor, not just to summon a party leader, but to summon a person who can command the support of his party and of a majority in parliament. It also illustrates the effective use a party can make of a Lieutenant-Governor in this situation. It is the party's responsibility to pick its leader and parliament's to sustain him. But it is in the interest of good government and of the party for the governor to check whether the party had really expressed itself. Mr. Gagnon, who evidently did not do so with sufficient thoroughness, got a choice from a group of ministers of a defunct cabinet which had been approved by a caucus, and, as Mr. Barrette himself revealed in his memoirs, the choice had been hesitant and doubtful. The result was uncertain leadership, divided loyalties, defeat in an election, party intrigue, and the leader's resignation. A similar result occurred in 1943 following a recommendation of retiring premier Mitchell Hepburn that Lieutenant-Governor Albert Matthews call on Gordon Conant to form a government–a choice which the Liberal party of Ontario refused to accept.

A remedy for uncertainty is sometimes suggested as being the selection of an interim premier pending the calling of a party convention. This alternative is not easy, because being an interim premier may be considered an unfair advantage to a possible candidate for leadership. The concern of prominent Republicans in 1973 over whether a new vice president might secure an advantage in the next presidential race illustrated how sensitive politicians are about this situation. What may happen if the interim premier changes his mind and becomes a candidate was indicated in 1954 by the turmoil in the Liberal party in Nova Scotia following Angus L. Macdonald's death, when Harold

Conolly, the interim premier, undertook not to run and changed his mind.[2] Difficulty also arose in 1968 when Robert Stanfield recommended G.I. Smith as interim premier. ". . .this was just on a temporary basis," said R.A. Donahoe, who also had hopes, "but temporary basis be damned."[3] A deputy premier has also been proposed, but he too has a disadvantage. In a difficult situation there is no guarantee he can command the support his deceased leader did. Furthermore, a collective choice may not be a concensus of individual choices, a situation dramatically illustrated in England by the passing over of R.A. Butler for the prime ministership on two occasions when "everybody" expected him to be chosen while individuals and groups in his own party worked against him; and by the selection of Senator George McGovern by a U.S. convention in 1972 when emotion obscured the fact his party would not rally behind him.

Those who would advise a governor in such emergencies should tell him, for their party's sake as well as the sake of the government, exactly what the situation is. He might then consult people within the party, as many constitutional sovereigns and presidents do, and make sure the person he summons actually has the necessary support. He would then tell the person of the existence of doubt, and request him to sound out his friends individually before accepting an invitation to form a government on the basis of an uncertain choice. This arrangement works well in other systems; there is no reason why it should not be suitable in Canada if a premier were to die suddenly.

A second emergency involves dismissing a government. A governor always relieves a government of its duties. In normal times the action is already determined by parliament or the people, the government acquiesces in the decision, and all the governor has to do is receive the prime minister and accept his resignation. But in abnormal circumstances a prime minister may flout the constitutional apparatus and attempt to remain in office despite it, and someone is needed to restrain him before it is too late. All dictators arise in such times. And disciplined political parties may support them. In Canada, where few will admit the presence of party subservience, the constitutional gymnastics of Mackenzie King and William Aberhart, described elsewhere,* now so controversial, were at the time supported blindly and unanimously by the parties concerned. "What's the constitution

---

*See pp. 129 and 134.

among friends?" was all one premier could reply when I asked how he justified an extraordinary tactic.

The possibility of this question being the cause of a confrontation between a governor and prime minister over the use of the dismissal power is now fortunately remote in Canada. The power can therefore be left in case Canada should have one of those serious constitutional upsets experienced elsewhere when a prime minister can take over unhindered control of the constitution as well as the government. The power is safe where it is, as a deterrent to the prime minister who is not likely to provoke it, and as an ultimate weapon for the governor who is in no position to use it without the most extreme provocation.

If use is not likely, threatened use may be practical after extreme provocation. Like disallowance and reservation of assent, the dismissal power hovers like a ghost to be summoned by a governor or invoked by a people, more to give the government a fright than to actually dismiss it. A premier who is in no position to call a governor's bluff by appealing to the legislature or the people will have to pay attention. The power hung like a spirit over Newfoundland at the end of the Smallwood era. It actually caused official fright in Manitoba in 1915 when it was conjured up by Lieutenant-Governor D.C. Cameron. The government of Sir Rodmond Roblin was involved in a scandal over construction contracts, and the premier tried to prevent the setting up of a Royal Commission to investigate. Cameron threatened to dismiss Roblin to force the government to set up the commission; and the subsequent revelations of impropriety resulted in the premier's resignation. Comparison with the Watergate affair, where in the absence of such a threat a crisis of frightful proportions became inevitable, illustrates the need for some warning or threat. So does the fall of any president where there is no-one of stature to force him to realize the seriousness of his situation. Votes of want of confidence or impeachment may not be reliable or practical because of a disciplined party majority in the one instance and lengthy cumbersome proceedings in the other. A threat can bring more immediate and less troublesome response. But such a threat must have a power behind it, however improbable its use may be. This is why the dismissal power remains almost inaccessible in the upper atmosphere of Canada's government.

The power to refuse dissolution has long been a favorite topic of discussion in Canada, and the King-Byng issue is her outstanding political drama. Section VI of the letters-patent provides the setting: "We do further authorize and empower Our Governor General to exercise all powers lawfully belonging to Us in respect of summoning, proroguing or dissolving the Parliament of Canada." The prime minister advises on the use of this power, and, as far as we know, it is nearly fifty years since the Governor General has exercised it on his own initiative by refusing dissolution. A similar situation prevails in the provinces, and the last known refusal by a Lieutenant-Governor took place in 1882. Authorities have enumerated known refusals. There may have been others.

This power is in the same inaccessible upper atmosphere where the others are, and all comments made on the others apply to it, including that on the importance of a threatened use. The latter may be of special value when legislatures cease to exercise much real power in the face of executive dominance.

Two practical aspects of the power of dissolution are important. One is its place in Canada's system of parliamentary elections. The other is the unwritten directions it gives to prime ministers.

We have noted that Canada's arrangements for parliamentary elections give the prime minister the right to decide when elections are to take place within parliament's maximum term of five years. The fixed parliamentary term has not been tried; and experience elsewhere indicates that it results in too long campaigns, adjustment of too much public business to an arbitrary distant date, and excessive emphasis on "lame duck" incumbents. When the date of dissolution is uncertain and secret until it is announced, people can only speculate, affairs of state proceed normally until the last moment, and the idea of "lame ducks" rarely takes hold. Governments may call elections, and oppositions may force them, should appeals to the public be desired. During preparations for an election the advantages are usually evenly divided between government and opposition. The former turns on the publicity and steps up the public works. The latter, without the pressures of office, can start a campaign earlier and make the most lavish promises. Unlike other arranged contests, elections enable the challengers to pick the weapons in the form of criticisms. To be fair we let the challenged pick the date. It is difficult, as we have said, to imagine Canadians putting the privilege of choosing the date in a written constitution–this would seem like too much power for a prime minister. So we slip it to him indirectly through the Governor General.

If the prime minister by himself could choose the date there could easily be an imbalance in the advantages enjoyed by both sides in an election. He could carry arbitrary misuse of the power to extremes, as heads of other governments have done. For example he could readily use a tactic mentioned by many Canadian constitutional authorities–subject the country to a series of dissolutions until he got his way. We therefore permit him as a participant in the election to say only "ready! set!", and then rely on the governor, with a hasty look around to ensure that all is well, to say "fire!"

The unwritten direction for the prime minister is to take care that all is well. Delay in saying "fire!" can only be tolerated in a democratic parliamentary system if all is not well, and none of the participants can do anything about it. That Canada has had so few issues involving this power is due not only to changes in the governor's power, but also to the effective obligation placed on the prime minister to be scrupulous.

That the prime minister may not be scrupulous can be made evident by yet another description of the King-Byng issue. A great drama like the sinking of the *Titanic*, it was not just a happening, but a warning and an example of what to avoid in the future. Certainly any governor or prime minister tempted to use or provoke emergency powers is bound to refer to it, and is likely to be influenced by it.

Mr. Mackenzie King, in power with a slim majority from 1921 to 1925, asked the people for a good majority in the election of 1925. The people refused his request, and returned 116 Conservatives, 101 Liberals, 24 Progressives, two Independents, and two Labor. Despite this result, Mr. King remained in office until parliament met, as was his right. Support of the Progressives then enabled him to carry on. A scandal involving the customs department developed early in 1926, and in June a vote of censure against the government was introduced and debated. The prime minister abruptly asked Governor General Lord Byng for a dissolution, and argued that he was automatically entitled to it as His Excellency's adviser. Lord Byng, fully aware that Mr. King was actually running away from a decision of the House on the customs scandal, and that the Conservatives with a larger number of seats than the Liberals had not had a chance to form a government, refused to grant the dissolution.[4] King resigned. Byng called on Arthur Meighen, leader of the Conservatives. Meighen formed a government.

129

A drama rivalling Gilbert and Sullivan then took place. The new government could be composed only of ministers without portfolio and Meighen had to give up his seat, because of a procedure followed before 1931 which required new ministers to resign and run in by-elections.* The Progressives got confused by this manoeuvre, and by King's criticism of "interference" by Byng and "unsurpation" by Meighen, and they waffled. Even then the Meighen government was only barely defeated in the House when one member broke his pair with another member who was absent and voted by mistake when he had agreed not to. Mr. Meighen thereupon asked for and obtained a dissolution. Byng and Meighen were made to seem like villains in the following election, and Mr. King won his majority.

The nuances of this issue have been admirably described by Dr. Eugene Forsey,[5] and carefully dissected by other authorities. The debate on who should have done what still goes on, and it provides the best available topic for discussion in political science classes in Canadian government. It would make a great Canadian folk opera! For our purposes there are several important features. The electors had not spoken clearly on any party's behalf; Mr. King's leadership was in question within his own party; parliament was in disarray; the King government, which had neither a majority nor a plurality, was under investigation by parliament and its support was in doubt. Therefore Mr. King was not scrupulous in presenting his request to the Governor General, and was in fact inviting the use of the power to refuse dissolution. On the other hand, the Governor General, put in a difficult position, did not rely on the fact that the people's verdict on the prime minister's act would have been decisive had the Conservatives won the election. As for Mr. Meighen, he could

---

*When a prime minister selected his cabinet before 1931, the new ministers had to resign their parliamentary seats and be elected again in by-elections. The theory was that the public thereby approved of members taking salaried seats in the cabinet, despite the fact that members of parliament could not take offices of emolument under the Crown. This arrangement, obviously inconvenient at any time, was disastrous for Meighen, because the absence of his ministers would cut down his small majority in the House until they could be elected again. He appointed them acting ministers to avoid the procedure, but this quite legal act was treated with scorn by Mr. King and suspicion by enough other members to defeat the government. The procedure no longer operates.

have done nothing else but accept the Governor General's request. As for the voters, they made a serious error in allowing titillating details of alleged and unfounded legal impropriety to overshadow the flouting of parliament that led to the issue.

There are too many "ifs" in this issue to permit decision on what might have been. But it does indicate the need for the power to refuse dissolution, because a prime minister may provoke its use against parliament on a far more serious occasion. Prime ministers have done worse elsewhere. It also indicates that both prime minister and Governor General must be aware of their closeness to the point where circumstance might justify refusal. The one is wrong if he gets too close to the point; the other is wrong if he is not close enough. That this lesson has not been lost on subsequent leaders has been the beneficial result of this actual appearance of an old ghost.

There is nothing undemocratic about this appearance, when the governor observes the limitations of his office. Indeed the governor may be stoutly defending democracy against a premier who seeks to circumvent it. He may also be doing the people a service by preventing chaos in their affairs brought on by a careless or desperate premier. Lieutenant-Governor Sir James Aikins of Manitoba refused to accept the resignation of Premier T.C. Norris and "recommendations for dissolution" in 1922, after a vote of non-confidence had been introduced. He instructed Norris to continue until supply had been voted and the sessional business finished. "Without his firm lead," says one authority, "a confusion bordering on anarchy would probably have resulted."[6] Insofar as conclusions can be drawn from such issues, they are that governors must be careful and that premiers should observe their own constitutional limitations.

Why premiers should observe them is too often neglected when commentators concentrate on a difference between premier and governor. The difference usually results originally from some breach or neglect of the rules in the continuing party contest in parliament that cannot be resolved in normal ways. The governor steps in on those rare occasions, not to interfere with the government, but to interpret the rules over which contending parties are by now hotly contesting. "In any contest, athletic or otherwise," said Mr. Michener, "where two parties are contending for power as political parties do, there must be a referee; and I think that we're fortunate in having inherited this constitutional system which provides the referee to see that the rules of the game are observed by those elected to govern."[7] But this is only half the matter. Even though the governor has to do nothing at all, he is still reinforcing the rules, because his presence and ultimate power deter the premier from going too far.

Another issue has had a lasting beneficial impact in reinforcing the rules of the game. It involved the refusal of a Governor General to make appointments on the advice of a government. Prime Minister Sir Charles Tupper was defeated in the general election of 1896, but between the election and his resignation he recommended appointments to Governor General Lord Aberdeen. Aberdeen refused to make them on the ground that the people had rejected Tupper. Circumstances had reached the point described earlier; the appointments would be final, and neither parliament nor people could do anything about them. The appointees would not have secured their posts by a responsible democratic process. And fairness was also involved. The defeated Conservatives had been in office continuously for eighteen years, and the bench and Senate were almost full of their nominees. The elected Liberals could now have a chance to redress the balance. The impact of this issue has been salutary. As far as we know, succeeding Governors General have not had to refuse appointments, not because the power is obsolete, but because, with one known exception, its use had not been provoked.* Prime ministers usually make their appointments before elections, and when they neglect to do it and are defeated, like Mr. St. Laurent in 1957, they know they should let the appointments lapse.

There are numerous descriptions of other issues cited by constitutional authorities in discussions about the Governor General and the Lieutenant-Governor. These accounts go back before Confederation and have left few stones unturned. Nevertheless, with rare exceptions**, writers tend to emphasize the changes in the governors' powers without discussing either what a prime

---

*The exception occurred in 1921 after the defeat of the Meighen government. The prime minister recommended to Lord Byng an appointment to a salaried office of a member of parliament which would open a seat for Meighen who had been defeated. Lord Byng accepted the advice with reluctance. Mr. King, the incoming prime minister, denounced Meighen's action as "high handed", "unwarranted", and "morally indefensible".[8]

**Like Eugene Forsey and R.I. Cheffins.

minister might do if they did not exist, or how a prime minister is deterred from mischief by the fact they do exist. Many writers also tend to ignore the probability of unknown instances. Some premiers may have asked for dissolution, for example, and been refused, or have sounded out governors and got a negative reaction, and then have kept quiet about the matter because they knew they were wrong. In numerous interviews I have heard the phrase "sounding out" a governor so often that I suspect the existence of a substantial number of instances that comon sense prevented from becoming issues. The emergency powers should therefore be considered in this light. As for the future, governors can only be successful Othellos if their advisers refuse the tempting role of Iago. And democratic parliamentary government, as vulnerable at times as Desdamona, can now be destroyed more readily by an advice-giver than by a possessor of power.

We must look beyond the constitutional issues for instances when a governor acts in a regulatory fashion. We have noted the consulting functions, most of which involve routine matters, and all of which depend on the personal relations between governors and advisers. Some of these functions become exercises of emergency power when problems of a most serious kind arise and a governor is the only person who can help the search for a solution. He does not solve the problems, it must be emphasized, he helps the search for solutions, which for him is much the more effective and permissible action. This action enables him, in the words quoted earlier about Lord Alexander, "to assist in making the business of running the country a success."

An emergency may arise when a permier is wrong and stubborn. It is astonishing how often heads of government rely on their own intuition, neglect to seek advice from colleagues–perhaps even discourage it, act in secret, indulge in wishful thinking, and expect everyone to accept the results. If a cabinet is docile, as several cabinets have been in Canada, the premier may actually run a one-man government.

This situation may work well when the premier is right, especially if he should have a weak cabinet or untrustworthy colleagues. The situation is serious if the premier is wrong. A good cabinet, or a few sound ministers in a weak cabinet, may keep him properly informed and check his impulsiveness. But even a premier of the highest calibre may not be easily controlled by his colleagues, and occasions arise of such seriousness that his stubbornness, or the assumed protection of his charisma, may lead to

133

dangerous situations. A distinguished governor may do wonders in this situation in several ways. The premier may ask and get advice that he would not take from colleagues. Ministers may quietly in a roundabout way ask the governor to convey discreetly to the premier some idea or warning that they would not dare present. And groups and individuals, of whom the governor sees many in his daily work, especially when he travels, may give him information, or indicate problems of which the premier is unaware or needs a reminder. All these situations are common in Canada.

In extreme circumstances this kind of consultation may be a desirable and effective restraint and a great public benefit. One example is a common problem in government which has been devastating in several countries. It is the accession of administrations new to power that were caused, not by the normal operation of public opinion, but by some special upheavals. These new inexperienced governments are sometimes egotistical and naive in their interpretations of their mandates, and may have little patience with long-term requirements. They may call their predecessors misguided and their opponents reactionary. They foresee a new era, and feel they know the way to the promised land. They may be impatient with existing rules, and angered at any suggestion they might not be men of destiny, sure-footed in the ways of statecraft, and guided unerringly by the will of the people, perhaps even by divine revelation. At such times they may need some restraint, or at least some recital of the facts of public life. This help is certainly good for the people's business, but it is also good for the new regime which forgets how short-lived such administrations may be, and how catastrophic are headlong and headstrong flights into the maelstroms of power.

There is no reason why Canadians should not undergo this experience, and, if they do, there is every reason why a governor should at least attempt to advise, especially if he is the only one who can do it. In one instance, that of Lieutenant-Governor J.C. Bowen of Alberta in 1937, he went further, and restrained Premier Aberhart from a foolhardiness involving his controversial Social Credit legislation which his party and successor never repeated during a long tenure of office. One can tangle with constitutional questions of who did or should have done this and that. The fact remains that a new, inexperienced provincial government introduced and pressed highly inflammable legislation without consulting other Canadian governments which were bound to react negatively, and imposed new and controversial matters, even ideas that conflicted with civil rights, without adequate reference to experienced experts or public opinion, without even taking the advice or enlisting the confidence of its own attorney-general. This was a real emergency of a kind that has so often been catastrophic. No governor wants to get involved in one. But he can do his best to prevent it by reacting privately. That may work; or at least it might set the premier thinking. If it does not work, the governor can either intervene formally or let the premier have his way. As far as the people's business is concerned, the fact that some consulting and restraining apparatus operates may do much good in a highly controversial situation.*

There are many less spectacular issues where, to alter Sherlock Holmes' phrase, the governor did not bark, indicating, perhaps, an "inside job". Actually the constitution gives him little chance to bark, but political realities make it desirable for him to growl occasionally. It is an advantage to governors and governments that nobody else can hear the growl, and to the people that he should growl when extreme circumstances require.

The consulting functions, particularly of the emergency type, can only be exercised in secrecy and confidence if they are to be democratic aids to government. Citizens are wrong if this secrecy leads them to believe that governors are just figureheads and rubber stamps. Good ones are more like responsible political oracles who see much, know much, and say nothing official unless one man advises them. They may whisper a few things discreetly to other officials. They may speak out loud on non-controversial and non-political matters. But the keys to their official opinions are entrusted to the premiers. How often these keys are used depends on the prime ministers who name them, on the premiers who are responsible for their actions, and on themselves, their abilities, and their common sense.

---

*While this book was in press Governor General Sir John Kerr of Australia dismissed Prime Minister Gough Whitlam on November 11, 1975 after a serious parliamentary deadlock and called on Malcom Fraser to form a government. Sir John gave his reasons in a public statement. (*Times*, London, Nov. 12, 1975.) In the general election which followed on December 14 the new government was returned with a large majority.

EIGHT

DECORATIVE FUNCTIONS

THE COLOUR of government tends everywhere to be drab, unless something is done about it. Government needs decoration to brighten it. Most of its functions become monotonous to perform and dull to watch. They need ceremony to appear interesting. Many governmental negotiations are difficult because officials are difficult. They require attentions and entertainment to soothe and stimulate the participants. Decorative functions are therefore exercised in all governments from primitive tribal councils to modern states, and they are inevitable. Each system picks its own particular forms, and uses them to create images and facilitate operations. The main problems are to pick the harmless forms of decoration, and to stage the show well enough to make it effective.

The duties of the Queen, Governor General, and Lieutenant-Governors include the decorative functions to facilitate the conduct of public business. The functions are entrusted to these officials because, as we have noted in Chapter Two, it is dangerous to allow politicians to exercise them; and they are handled better by people whose job it is to perform them.

Canadians have tended recently to be shy and hesitant in

their attitudes to decorative functions. This is extraordinary. There was no shyness in either their French or British heritage, which featured some of the world's best practical decorative functions in government. The environment cannot be the cause. The first Canadians had splendid tribal rites and entertainments. The first white settlers brightened their strenuous lives with activities that make modern affairs seem dull by comparison. Champlain's Order of Good Cheer was a most practical society at a time of tragedy. Canada was founded by statesmen who relieved the strain of their business with colour, and part of their success was due to the colour. If heritage and environment are not the causes, perhaps it is the influence of the next-door neighbours. There is a streak of political puritanism among Americans that creeps out from their many assets. The United States has generally had a wealthy, expanding economy, and the resulting materialism may have dulled their collective sense of political humour and thus their government. Their public stimulus tends to be sensationalism rather than decoration, and the costly result is an erratic, and often ineffective, series of impacts on the nation and the world. Modern Canadians perhaps try to mix these outlooks in their practices with pallid results.

Nevertheless, Canadians can put on a good show when they want to, and they obviously enjoy doing so. But they do not let on. They quarreled about their nation's centennial, delayed preparations until the last minute, and then had a wonderful time. They had rows in every province over the construction of cultural centres, and then regarded them as major community assets. They sneered when the Quebec Winter Carnival and Stratford Festival were founded by a few venturesome souls, and then packed them and advertised them to the world. They laughed when the Group of Seven painted for them the very colour and atmosphere of Canada, later to honour the painters and run up the prices of the works to astronomical figures. The same conflicting attitudes appear in the decorative functions of government.

Canadians obviously enjoy these functions when they permit themselves to do it. But uncertainty may be caused by a feeling of frivolity, which to some may seem irrelevant in government. There is nothing frivolous or irrelevant about it. The purposes served by decorative functions in Canada are the same as those served by similar functions in all governments, and they are inseparable from public affairs. One is show; the other is the conduct of business. Both purposes are as old as government itself. They are the same now as they were in the days of Pericles who, wrote Plutarch, "let loose the reins to the people. . .contriving continually to have some great public show or solemnity, some banquet, or some procession. . .to please them."[1]

The show is carried on at three levels in Canada. The Queen's tours are major occasions which only a sovereign's presence can provide. Official ceremonies, visits to institutions, and other events give opportunities to thousands of citizens to see a world figure who represents centuries of political tradition, national sovereignty, and contemporary international friendship. The Governor General's activities do not evoke emotions as strongly as the Queen's presence does. Nevertheless they do stimulate a national community spirit, and symbolize the common heritage shared by all the provinces. The image conveyed tends to be constitutional; enthusiasm for the individual is properly modest. Respect is what the Governor General receives, and the impact of his work rests on his identity as the one non-political personality at the summit of the federal government, and on his association with the traditions of government as the representative of the Crown. The Lieutenant-Governor's activities evoke reactions similar to those of the Governor General. He carries the show to the grass roots—the local celebrations, prize-givings, and openings of community enterprises. By any comparison, this three-scale impact of the state's identity and the people's heritage is one of the most efficient in the world when full advantage is taken of it.

The significance of this system to the citizens is two-fold—what it provides them directly, and what it does in the conduct of their public business.

What citizens generally see is the spectacle. An appearance by the Queen, Governor General, or Lieutenant-Governor, if properly staged, is an impressive public-relations event for government itself, not for *a* government. It is these auspices that no state can afford to do without. It is a serious mistake to relate the event to the adulation of an individual. It is what the individual represents that is honoured. It is also a mistake to think the visitor is being given special entertainment. It is the public that is being entertained. It is hard work for the person concerned, and she or he is not doing it for vanity. The twenty-fifth parade and fiftieth reception are as much routine as any citizen's daily stint at the office, except that the principal guest and what she or he wears, does, and says are the subjects of every onlooker's scrutiny and of every reporter's commentary.

It is an equally serious mistake to take a puritan attitude to the events, as if there were something indecent or undemocratic about a populace enjoying a public spectacle. Humans will have their spectacles and will enjoy them, and pay huge sums for them, from the idolizing of film stars to the patronizing of blue movies, from the hallucinations provided by drink and drugs to the emotions released by riots and wars. Spectacles may even offend every canon of human decency. Three hundred citizens of Florida made headlines around the world in 1973 as they cheered a woman climbing a tower to commit suicide, shouted to her to jump, and assaulted the firemen and police who rescued her.[2] Countless similar forms of spectacle *are* both indecent and undemocratic, and are many times more costly to society than the useful spectacles associated with the Crown. It is even more mistaken still to regard crown events as snobbery. Such a criticism is almost always inverted snobbery, which is highly dangerous. It not only features puritanism, a lack of sense of humour, and a dog-in-the-manger outlook, but also neglects the existence of much more troublesome forms of snobbery in other activities. It is the wrong word to use anyway.

The right word is celebrity. Regardless of what people may say, they like celebrity in everything they do, and, with rare exceptions, will seek it themselves. Farmers, hockey players, writers, rose growers, union organizers, politicians, and everyone else rush to acclaim leaders in their fields of interest, and, if they can, to get some kudos for themselves. Well known books like Vance Packard's *The Status Seekers* and *The Pyramid Climbers* reveal how general is Western society's liking for celebrity. And, despite theory, it is just as obvious in communist and third-world countries as it is in the West. Indeed the logic of celebrity-hunting is rarely explainable, as any community can see. Let it arrange simultaneous visits by a movie starlet and a Nobel-prize winner and watch who gets the bigger and more costly reception.

There is nothing "wrong" about celebrity; it is natural, except when carried to excess. Much of it outside of public life is also expensive. The public not only likes it, but demands it, as anyone quickly finds out who promotes literature by "name" authors, features a professional "personality", counts the newspaper columns devoted to the Taylor-Burton marriage, or assesses the enormous business in gossip magazines. By any comparison, crown activity is low-priced and useful, especially by one comparison. A state will have its celebrity in some form anyway, and it is healthy to have the form provided by representatives of the Crown because it is politically harmless.

Canada illustrates all these matters. Celebrity and the colour which accompanies it are everywhere, from acclaim for the first baby born in a new year to the showering of expensive gifts on the one-millionth customer at a store. A beauty queen may cost Canadians more in her year's reign than a Lieutenant-Governor. A football team may cost more than a Governor General. An Eaton's Santa Claus parade, which citizens pay for as consumers, is more lavish and costly than the opening of parliament. The colour and cost involved in patronizing and policing the lively establishments on Yonge Street make the cost of activities at Rideau Hall and the government houses seem modest. So do the bands, hand-outs, performers, and hospitality suites which are now colourful and expensive features of party conventions. In public and business administrations, it is not difficult to note the elements of celebrity in the form of empire building, its cost, and its comparatively low usefulness.[3]

As for citizens themselves, anyone inclined to be critical of public ceremonial or of "dressing up", regalia, rank and degree, titles of honour, protocol, visits of potentates, and the like, should note the enormous numbers of Canadians involved in organizations such as the Knights of Columbus and the Masonic Lodge, in which the most ancient of ceremonial, including the Shriners' rituals which are derived from Arab countries, has been featured and enjoyed as a regular part of the activities. And no citizens follow such customs more assiduously than young people. They may call themselves leftists, reformers and the like, and celebrate Chairman Mao, Che Guevera, or Ho Chi Minh, or wear Indian head bands, Afro haircuts, granny glasses, and long dresses from the last century. They may be obedient to protocol and rip the bottoms of jeans and sew patches on the seats at the dictates of some distant, anonymous arbiter. They may adopt colourful language or accept trendy and expensive fashions from public relations experts who reach the headlines, and from flashy, costly magazines that cater to fashionable activities, racy pastimes, and colourful issues. Many join religious sects that feature gurus and most elaborate ritual imported from other lands. Even man's basic functions are subjected to contemporary ritual, as eating and drinking are surrounded by ceremonial and fashion, and sex is the subject of a collosal literature of illustration and advice as old "hang-ups" are replaced by new ones.

It seems strange, therefore, that critics could suggest that celebrity and colourful activities are inappropriate in Canada's public life, when elsewhere they feature them, indeed seek them avidly. It seems dangerous too, because if colour in public life is rejected in one era, government may appear too dull in the next, and attract one of those periodic invaders of democracy, a powerful demagogue, a mesmeric dictator, or military regime that will promise the people a good show. "To say," wrote Confucius, "as people often do, that ritual is all very well so long as it is not used as an instrument of government, is wholly to misunderstand the purpose of ritual."[4]

The spectacle provided by the Queen, Governor General, and Lieutenant-Governors gives an opportunity to citizens to enjoy a public show and to salute someone who represents all of them as citizens. Politicians represent some of them as voters when they are involved in spectacles at election time. Other people represent them as sports enthusiasts, movie-goers, novel-readers, and the like. It is Canada or a province of Canada that the Queen and the governors represent, and every Canadian is part of both political units. The meaning of this association is what the Queen and the governors emphasize to Indian Canadians, boy scouts, patients in a hospital, miners, elderly folk, or fathers standing on curbs with small children on their shoulders. Even if most of these citizens have no interest in governmental powers or constitutional issues, they know something is happening that concerns their state and that is common to all Canadians.

This kind of show is not just designed for crowds. Its impact on individuals is equally important. It is remarkable to watch what happens to a person who has been engaged in conversation by the Queen during a walkaround; to a boy who receives a medal for bravery from the Governor General; or to a farmer who shows off the fine points of a cow to the Lieutenant-Governor at a county fair. These contacts are not just casual formalities; they make deep impacts on many people in all walks of life. Indeed these contacts may be for countless citizens the only occasion when their state recognizes them without asking for their votes or their taxes.

There is still another direct benefit to the citizens which this spectacle provides. It helps them in community planning. Everyone knows that having a party at home encourages a family to clean the house and do necessary painting and repairs. It often takes an occasion to prompt a desirable but indefinitely postponed action. We behave the same way in communities. Countless parks, memorials, scholarships, and physical improvements, as well as successful commemorations, were the direct results of crown visits that have remained afterwards for the benefit and pleasure of citizens. When one counts the number of these projects in every part of Canada, the result is staggering.

Of all citizens, the children receive the most benefit. They like celebrities, especially if there is something heroic about them. Governors General have been successful in bringing a sense of wonder and national feeling to young Canadians. And many Lieutenant-Governors have aroused youthful enthusiasm in their provincial traditions. Most of them have also conveyed ideas related to moral values, responsibility, education, and other attributes of citizenship. Visits from men who represent the state, accompanied by bands, guards of honour, and waving flags are unmatched in this respect by any other occasions. And the impressions remain in young memories as about the only non-political symbol which illustrates what children read in school books. How long these impressions remain depends on how well the show is staged. A perfunctory visit put on by unskilled local worthies who get in the way is shabby. A contrived event managed by local education officials will disillusion the youngsters. It is tragic to see how such people can kill all the benefits for both governors and participants. A community is wise to entrust arrangements to those who know how to put on a good show. The impact on teen-agers and young people is also great, if the contact with them is carried out with the same amount of care exercised by very rich pop singers and professional athletes who know how to use PR. Anyone who watched J.J. Bowlen of Alberta in action knows how effective a governor's contact with young people can be.

Good governors are not back-slapping personalities. They do not have to be. Their own attributes are reinforced by the dignity of the Crown, and if these attributes are effective the combination is powerful. The dignity alone will not support a weak governor, although it will help him to muddle through. An overly-hearty manner will make him appear superficial. But a Georges Vanier can make an enormous impact with dignity because his manner matched it. And a D.L. MacLaren of New Brunswick can

142

make a similar impact with a spectacular manner that never offended his dignity. This combination impresses any citizen, but it is particularly effective among young people.

This effectiveness does require, for all citizens, a show that is worth watching and remembering. It is misguided seriousness and careless arrangements that weaken public interest. There is nothing democratic about drabness, or egalitarian about unobtrusiveness. There is nothing snobbish about a Windsor uniform, or irrelevant about a guard of honour. No national or provincial image is created or concept of egalitarianism catered to by apologetically slipping a governor into a crowd, or giving the impression that he is just one of the boys. It is not he personally that is being elevated and honoured, but the representative of the entire state. Indeed, when the local show is not good enough people will turn to the *gloire* of a de Gaulle or the glamour of a Kennedy, buy by the millions novels on the exploits of Napoleon and the amorous adventures of Henry VIII, or pay homage to the stars of entertainment and sport who, at public expense, are given remuneration, publicity, and tribute that any governor would envy. History, human nature, and personal achievement are not highlighted by drabness, and the spirit of a state or province must seek some expression through cheer in the hearts and lumps in the throats. "It was a grand sight," says one observer of Canadian governors, in putting this matter in its real perspective, "democracy in gold lace and feathers, but real democracy nevertheless. I just cannot get used to the governors I see these days, governors in business suits and Stetsons who treat me as a civic equal. I am spoiled in the matter of governors. I like them old, white-haired, dignified, with plumed aides beside them, and cannon firing salutes in the distance."[5]

The second important aspect to citizens of the decorative functions of the Crown is their influence on the conduct of public business.

Citizens should understand that public business can be boring to those in charge of it unless there is some official relief from routine. Even the few men who wield real power need to be taken out of their offices to mix with others in convivial, dignified, official surroundings. Otherwise they become too serious, and that is when they become dangerous. "I think," Premier Alexei Kosygin of the Soviet Union told the Canadian Manufacturers Association on the virtues of conviviality, "it would be best if ministers could meet more often, have lunch together, maybe drink vodka together and maybe think less about fighting."[6] The great majority of public officials in any system are destined to have little power and influence, and none of the excitements of important participation and responsibility. They need convivial, dignified, official surroundings even more, to give them a sense of involvement or an opportunity to meet "celebrities", and their wives something to do and talk about. As for most citizens who are not in government, major occasions provide contacts with officials that are far more fruitful than other opportunities, such as reading Hansard or sitting in legislative galleries, neither of which is of great interest to the public. Provision must therefore be made for the fact that people close to government are human. If it is not, they will succumb to puritanism which is deadly in government, or seek less effective outlets elsewhere.

Decorative functions as aids to governing are provided in various forms to influence the human characteristics of politicians, officials, and citizens. These functions have existed everywhere from ancient to modern times for the same purposes and with successive generations of participants who do and say pretty much the same things. A Tito would understand what was happening, and why, could he have sat at Caesar's table; and a contemporary Confucius would be right at home in Rideau Hall. The ritual has remained in government for so long because it is human and it works.

The dinner at a government house is an example, which we should examine here to assess, not the dinner, but the human characteristics. It looks like entertainment, which it is; and for that reason alone it is useful. But it is also public business carried on in special circumstances. The host may invite a group of politicians of different parties, such as provincial premiers during a conference, members of a legislature at the beginning of a session, or a mixture of politicians and others, and they meet in a nonpartisan atmosphere with appropriate gastronomic accompaniments. The rivalry of the day is muted; dull routine is forgotten amidst candlelight and music; and conversation flows as the guests are soothed and humoured. Official rank and seniority tend to disappear as guests mingle and talk to others to whom they might elsewhere have no access. A premier, for example, may delight in being "one of the boys" at such a gathering; it is probably his only chance. All the rank tends to concentrate in the host, and premiers and ministers, like bishops when an archbishop is present, or trade union organizers when a union presi-

144

dent is on hand, are less official and more approachable in this kind of atmosphere.

This is a setting for developing official contacts and friendships, encouraging solutions of major problems, clearing up personal misunderstandings, making necessary compromises, and receiving essential agreements. The better the dinner and hospitality the more of this business will be done. Officials, particularly busy ones who carry great responsibility, are more amenable at a dinner table or on comfortable settees with good cigars and liquors, than at a conference table or in a legislature. They will not sit down to conduct business, but business will pop up in the conversation, and they will lower official barriers. Meanwhile, shrewd leaders and knowledgeable aides will do all kinds of useful things, like seating possible antagonists or unacquainted officials next to one another, manoeuvring two opposing potentates into the governor's study for a chat, and dropping facts and suggestions into receptive ears. The atmosphere is also good for assessing people. Wise men and fools reveal themselves here to a much greater extent than they do in a committee room or legislative chamber. And the resulting enjoyments, associations, and work are more useful than the hectic, casual, expensive, and tiring encounters of that fashionable but desperate other public gathering, the cocktail party

The feeling of being appreciated is an important goal of government house functions. The significance of compliments, toasts, and friendly conversation is obvious, although there are not many places in government where they are given and appreciated. It is a harmless form of flattery because it is a harmless place to give it. And there are many men who want, need, and avidly seek such attentions in public life. But humouring is only a part of appreciation. Recognition is more important. Many politicians and officials in both federal and provincial governments get little recognition, perhaps none whatever, and they get restless or discontented if they go ignored for too long. For able ones, there are not many rewards and opportunities for state appreciation, and a government house function provides a useful recognition. We should make no mistake. They want recognition; they look for it; they are resentful if they do not get it; and politics itself encourages them in this attitude. Anyone who doubts this should take responsibility for arranging public functions, and he will soon appreciate how many prima donnas there are in public life, how readily public life turns men into prima donnas, and how sensitive they and their wives are about such matters. But they are also sensitive in a positive way. The faithful politician or civil servant, and his wife, are grateful to be recognized on occasions that are important and unique enough to make them feel appreciated. As for expense, this appreciation costs the state less in a year than the official gives in tips to his barber. If he gets many such invitations, they are much cheaper than would be his tendency to use empire building as an alternative way of seeking appreciation and recognition.

For the politician or official who is less competent, a government house function is most welcome. The problem to be met with respect to him is status. He cannot be ignored, because he has the same official status as others in his category, and because he may represent an interest group that craves attention. But use of what talents he thinks he has may not be possible or desirable in the interest of parliament or the civil service, and he may not deserve recognition. Nevertheless, he must be kept content, and, for his sake, so must his wife, and, for the sake of harmony, so must his interest group. Ottawa and all provincial capitals must accommodate many such people. Memberships on committees or innocuous chores and junkets are helpful methods. A flutter of invitations is more useful and harmless. They recognize status in interesting ways, and are soothing balms for personal discontents and frustrations that might otherwise hamper government. It is obvious how happy these people are to be invited to government house. The host knows them or hears about them from his ministers and aides, and gives them a special handshake or word of greeting. Senior men present give them special notice not otherwise possible. Little confidences can be whispered in their ears, and special efforts can be made to ensure them and their wives a good time that will provide happy memories in dull days ahead, or stories they can pass on to constituents or friends as evidence of their places in the official sun.

Similar human factors justify other events, like luncheons, garden parties, and receptions, which recognize and humour citizens along with officials. Sometimes the total may seem irrelevant or expensive to a critic who sees it as a social clique. This view is wrong. In the first place politicians and officials behave in social ways no differently from other citizens. And their wives have the same social needs as other wives of busy men. In the second place, public men are elected or recruited from all parts of the country or province, and for many of them the capital is not home. Why should they not have a social environment in the capital? For them it is a society of people with a common task–governing. It is in the interest of the citizens that they should have hospitality from the state which they can enjoy, and which encourages cooperation among them. There is nothing undemocratic about it. Doctrinaires who disclaim a need for such activities wear their halos too tight. Should they be theoretical in their criticism and cite an egalitarian excuse, they should sample some of the spectacular hospitality of socialist, communist, and other governments which can no more do without such activity than Canadian governments can. Should they be mercenary in their criticism, they should note how much cheaper is a successful dinner than an unproductive meeting. Should they think the situation unique to politics, they can observe similar phenomena among professors and students, clergymen and parishioners, businessmen and employees and their customers, as well as among citizens in all walks of life.

The social and decorative functions also serve visiting officials and foreign diplomats. All nations use such functions as a means of encouraging personal contacts, exchanging information, paying respect to distinguished visitors, and providing entertainment and friendships for diplomats who spend most of their working lives away from home in a succession of temporary posts. The value of these relationships is enhanced, as we have noted, in a non-political setting that emphasizes ties between states in addition to associations between governments.

These functions are shared by countless citizens. The Governor General and the Lieutenant-Governors receive and entertain many thousands from all walks of life. From the Governor General's children's Christmas party to a Lieutenant-Governor's afternoon tea for a local Women's Institute, citizens share in the hospitality of the state. Any individual may call on New Year's Day to receive a handshake and refreshments, and he is thereupon invited back to some other function. Numerous groups that meet in the capitals include on their agendas a function at government house. This hospitality is a form of public relations for government itself, as distinct from a government; and its effects on citizens are similar to those on politicians.

The extent of this kind of public relations, and the number of citizens involved, can be appreciated by noting the activities of Governor General Michener. From April 1967 to January 1974 he made 203 official tours, travelled 267,758 miles, and delivered

522 speeches. He was also host at luncheons and dinners to 19,-994 people; at balls and dances to 6,587; at garden parties to 32,-158; and at receptions and levees to 50,468. In the same period 132,249 citizens visited the public rooms at Government House.[7] In addition to these contacts, the number of citizens whom His Excellency met at public functions outside Government House and while on tour must have made an impressive total.

It is important to repeat again that *state* functions, as distinct from ordinary official entertaining, should not be provided regularly in a democracy by a government, which they certainly would be in Canada if there were no governors. People too dependent on a government for state functions will permit that government to use the functions to advertise itself and maintain itself in power. A government that controls state functions tends to spend far more on them than the Crown does because it indulges in the expensive effort of inflating its own image. It also tends to use them to favour its own partisans, and is inclined to ignore the opposition and its supporters and citizens in whom it is not particularly interested. It is the state itself that should handle them, in the safest, non-partisan, and democratic manner. In any event, premiers and ministers have enough work of their own, and should not be encouraged to devote too much time and effort to all the decorative functions which governing demands.

The Queen, Governor General, and Lieutenant-Governors also go to citizens' entertainments, and, what is even better, give the citizens excuses for having community entertainments, which are much needed in a healthy society. Several engagements a day take them and their wives as guests to convention banquets, club celebrations, testimonial dinners, military gatherings, women's teas, college and school events, country fairs, and many other occasions. They also visit factories, mines, sporting events, hospitals, and the like, where they can meet many people and be seen by many more. These activities provide status for the events, which thus have the representatives of all the people bring to them the patronage of the state. This patronage also provides a colourful official whose presence can be put to many advantages, of which not the least is a boost in attendance. It is also financially profitable to hosts who put on events for charitable purposes, and have the state's representative or his wife as patron or honorary president. If the governors are good speakers they bring messages of national and provincial interest of a non-political nature to thousands of citizens.

All this is hard work. Anyone who thinks a conscientious governor lives in gilded splendour and luxurious idleness is wrong. He gets up early and retires late. In the interval he handles a large correspondence, keeps informed on official business, meets many people, mostly strangers whom he must impress with his interest in them, listens to numerous speeches, eats a varied diet that involves a risk of digestive difficulties, is on continuous good behaviour, travels much, and talks all the time. He needs strong legs, a tireless right arm, and endless patience to endure what becomes a gruelling routine. His wife is equally busy, but she has an added problem. She must dress well and look well, because she is on show, and citizens are not charitable if her looks do not please them.

The job must be well done to be appreciated. Some governors have been ineffective because they lacked the necessary skill, or because they allowed personal vanity to intrude in their official duty. Others have made enormous impacts because they succeeded in the three most important facets which are combined in all the decorative functions: theatre, entertainment, and mystique, each of which is only effective when well performed. These qualities are a necessary part of human relations in government. And they involve the governor, not as a person, but as the representative of the state. Indeed the impact may be so strong as to earn a judgement like that passed by one authority on Lieutenant-Governor R.F. McWilliams, for his "actions which have had a marked effect on the development of a closer sense of unity within Manitoba."[8]

Governments make use of these decorative functions of the Crown for their own purposes. They may ask a governor to recognize a group by entertaining its convention; honour a community or industry by paying it an official visit; feature a special message in a public speech; entertain a visitor; or pay special attention to a local individual. This kind of recognition helps get business done if any group or person is restless or annoyed, feels neglected, or must be put in good humour, be thanked for something, or be encouraged to do some public service. There are many occasions when governments are unable to make appropriate overtures or give proper recognition because of political implications, and so rely on a governor to create an atmosphere of good will of which they can take advantage. One successful politician, for example, became accustomed to receiving tough visitors for difficult business at three o'clock in the afternoon, and

149

softening them up beforehand by having them well entertained at lunch at the official residence. Shrewd premiers are good at this kind of thing, and governors are glad to help them out.

Governors are also frequently requested by citizens to provide similar functions for organizations and celebrations. Centennials are an example, and Canada has had many of them. It is a mistake for premiers and ministers to be too obvious at commemorative events because, with rare exceptions, they cannot shed their partisan images which should have no place on such occasions. A project may be spoiled if it is sponsored in a "look what your government is doing for you" atmosphere, especially if it is so associated with a government that the opposition criticizes it or a succeeding government ignores it. The appearance of a premier or minister invites local party stalwarts to turn the event into a rally, or to accompany it by a political meeting; such tactics turn attention away from the project. Cornerstones everywhere bear mute testimony to the extent to which politicians will use events to commemorate themselves. Only a rare one can honour a building with his name; most of them are soon forgotten, and the stone means nothing. Commemorative literature, ceremonies, and entertainments suffer from suggestions of governmental propaganda, especially if the opposition or other public organizations are overshadowed or ignored. Wise premiers know all this, and ensure the success of such occasions by subduing their politics so everyone can participate as citizens rather than as voters. If they use a governor as principal host or guest for most state events, and the Queen for grand occasions, the commemoration will enjoy more immediate success and lasting memories. And the government itself will get more credit.

This use of the Queen and the governors is by far the best and least expensive form of public relations. PR is big business, and governments spend millions on it. So do other organizations. If someone responsible for a public event considers the proposals and estimates of a PR firm, and then compares the cost of a plan featuring the Queen or a governor and the kind of events they sponsor and impact they make, he will find an enormous difference in effect and cost. For one ordinary event the firm may charge more than it costs to maintain a governor a whole year. For a major occasion, a centennial for example, the mere fact that the Queen accepts an invitation to attend provides free publicity on a national scale which would otherwise cost a province an enormous amount in advertising. If a government itself handles an event the cost is also high because politicians and civil servants are good at spending money on propaganda. Canadians are not generally aware, however, that they must pay for PR under any circumstances, and that their most active and least costly sources of it are Buckingham Palace and their government houses.

Similar considerations apply to events where governors are guests. Every public function seems to require a celebrity of some kind, and Canadians pay high fees for the mere presence of entertainers, athletes, and other "big names" who make fortunes on the celebrity circuit. Or they call on someone from that numerous breed, the guest speaker, for whom they pay fees and expenses. The governors, on the other hand, charge nothing. And it is no idle speculation to state that their presence is more democratic, if one feels the need to apply that word in assessing them, than that of the other celebrities. The speeches of some of them do not suffer in comparison, either in entertainment or in lasting impact. If a critical taxpayer wants to study the matter, let him compare his Lieutenant-Governor at ten dollars a plate and an itinerant hockey player at fifty.

This matter of cost has sometimes been raised by those who assess the Crown. They make two basic mistakes. It is not the Crown that costs money, but the functions, and they are inevitable. It is not the Queen or governors for whom the money is being spent, but the governments and the citizenry. How the decorative functions could otherwise be performed as well, as safely, and as cheaply is an important question which can be clearly answered. The experience of no other state indicates a better or less costly system.

Exact figures on the cost of the Crown are elusive because there are so many variables. Nevertheless, calculations yield a gross cost of approximately twelve cents per Canadian per year, a net cost of less than three cents, and, when all factors are considered, no real cost at all, but a substantial return to the taxpayers that yields them a profit.* The costs are inevitable. If there were

---

*By gross cost I mean the entire outlay charged in the public accounts to crown activities at all three levels. Net cost is what remains after deducting expenses attributable directly to public request or initiative. For example, if a governor spends one thousand dollars on a garden party for a Womens' Institute Convention, it is the group the money is being spent on, not the governor. The profit is illustrated in the follow-

no Queen, Governor General, and Lieutenant-Governor, their functions would still remain, and would have to be performed by other institutions at higher cost.

Nothing is spent by Canadians on the Queen or members of the royal family, except when they are invited to Canada for special events. For such visits expenses are arranged beforehand as part of the cost of the events, as they would be with any official or special guest. This expense is small in relation to the budgets of centennials and the like. The 320,000 dollars spent by the federal government on the Queen's tour of 1973, for example, was not a "cost" of the Crown, but a modest, and highly profitable, outlay in connection with several major events and celebrations in four provinces. It provided an enormous boost in significance and public interest; indeed, from a purely business standpoint, it made much more money for the places visited. The Queen and the Duke of Edinburgh did so much for the Calgary Stampede in 1973, that from the financial standpoint alone—aside from all the other considerations—it was no wonder that Premier Lougheed's announcement that they would be invited to the 1978 Commonwealth Games in Edmonton "was greeted by thunderous applause from MLA's."[9]

The Governor General's salary is $48,666.60, of which he spends much on his job. His expenses, including staff, residence, and travel, are about 1.3 million dollars. Like the Queen, he performs most of the functions at the invitation of governments and public organizations, and, by any comparison, this cost is trifling compared to the cost of the events and the contribution he makes to them and to the places he visits. As for the Lieutenant-Governors, until 1975 their salaries were 20,000 dollars in Ontario and Quebec, 16,000 dollars in Prince Edward Island, and 18,000 dollars in the other provinces. In 1975 the salaries were raised to 35,000 dollars in all provinces. They also received some federal assistance, varying from 10,000 dollars to 18,000 dollars, toward defraying the cost of travel throughout their provinces. And most of them also spend much of their own money. The provincial governments provide some additional allowances for special purposes, as well as residences in most provinces which are designed, not for the governor's convenience, but for local public

---

ing paragraph, and in comparison with expensive alternatives to crown participation in events and in the constitutional process.

events. The gross cost of the ten Lieutenant-Governors to the tax-payers is little more than one million dollars, of which about a tenth is spent on maintaining the incumbents (who pay income tax); the balance is spent on activities which governments and citizens ask them to perform.[10] These amounts are miniscule in the budgets of the governments concerned, and in comparisons with salaries of numerous citizens, and with the huge sums spent on public relations, celebrity worship, and fashions in entertainment.

We have seen that the decorative functions are only a part of the purpose of the Crown. For the same cost, all the other consti-tutional functions are being performed. To accommodate them in other ways is expensive. Not to accommodate them at all has proved ruinous. If ruinous seems too strong a word, we should re-member that many modern states have become legally, morally, and financially bankrupt because of the failures of government. The mere existence of the twelve persons representing the Crown, as well as their numerous functions, help to prevent failures and the huge costs which accompany them.

This preventive function helps other institutions. The enor-mous value of parliament and of the work and leadership of the competent among its members, the intricate powers of cabinets, the integrity of courts of justice, and the loyalty of the civil serv-ice and the military are essential to the effectiveness, indeed the very survival, of the democratic state. In an age when, as we have observed, democracy appears on the ebb in world politics and in-stability of political institutions is common, the reinforcements which the Crown provides the other institutions in Canada are efficient by any comparisons. And, at a time of expensive bu-reaucracy, the miniscule cost of the Crown, and the way it now operates in Canada, must surely compare favourably with other Canadian federal and provincial institutions.

But, as we have observed, "efficiency" is only one aspect of the matter. The other, represented by the decorative functions, concerns the spirit of the nation, the loyalty of citizens, public feeling for its traditions, and faith in its future. These vital ele-ments, obviously lacking in many states without a Crown, are difficult to establish and maintain if they depend on political leaders and parties, parliaments, and military establishments. They thrive on emotion, pleasure, and faith, and these cannot be forced, legislated, or administered without autocracy; if they are

153

so forced they are illusory and unstable. To encourage these elements is essential, and the Crown and its representatives are in a unique position to do it well.

It would be naive to assert that the Crown always succeeds. Like any other institution, it is sometimes misunderstood or ignored by citizens. Its image may be tarnished by a few unsuitable incumbents in its offices. And its efforts may be thwarted by political encroachments on what should be non-political functions. Nevertheless, few governmental institutions anywhere have adapted as well to changing constitutional circumstances, different incumbents, and political upheavals. Comparisons with alternatives abroad and other institutions in Canada illustrate that the Crown has no weaknesses which are unique to it and not inherent in government generally.

The Crown's functions are particularly valuable in maintaining that essential element so elusive in most countries—national unity. Canadians want national unity without having it forced by autocratic methods so common elsewhere. Yet they also want provincial, regional, and local diversity. These desirable but often conflicting wishes are difficult to maintain, and Canadians can go only part way to maintain them by legislation and agreements. Other means are necessary, and the Crown provides many of them. We should now examine the actual and potential contributions of the Crown to Canadian unity and diversity, and consider some of the problems involved which concern the Crown as well as all other Canadian institutions.

NINE

UNITY AND DIVERSITY

THE CROWN has been questioned in Canada in connection with the inevitable stresses of a federal state. This questioning has been understandable, not because the Crown has failed to serve Canadians, but because it has been the strongest link among all the provinces, from colonial days when they had nothing else in common, to the present when it remains the one non-political element at the summits of Canadian governments. Critics of federalism or of federal-provincial problems, and doctrinaires who seek to destroy the Canadian system, can strike at no more vital source of unity.

Assaults on unity are evident. Complaints of "alienation" have been made in all regions and by numerous groups. Quebec has a separatist party. Alberta has an Independent Alberta Association. This protest provokes questions about local sovereignty and national unity, particularly when times are good and separate identities seem for the moment to be viable, when there are quarrels over provincial jurisdiction and division of resources, when there are inadequate national efforts and symbols with which local interests may identify, and especially when the age-old concept of national self-determination is brought forth for argument.

Complaints about federalism have been common in all provinces. Criticism of the Crown has been particularly evident in Quebec. But only in recent years. It came up suddenly.* In 1939 King George VI received a tumultuous welcome in Quebec. Princess Elizabeth was enthusiastically received there in 1953. Eleven years later, however, Queen Elizabeth II's visit to Quebec was marred by disorder in the streets. Meanwhile the role of the Lieutenant-Governor of Quebec was downgraded. This change was certainly not the fault of the Queen, the Governor General, or the Lieutenant-Governor of Quebec. None had committed any indiscretion or interfered with any governmental process in Quebec. Nor had any powers of the Crown been imposed, or duties of the Crown been neglected. And Quebec City is the only place outside Ottawa where the Governor General has a residence. What happened? It is difficult to find a more reliable answer than that I heard from Governor General Vanier shortly after the 1964 episode. The Crown was in no way at fault, he said; it was being used as an object of criticism for political purposes; it was vulnerable to attack on national unity; it was one of Quebec's strongest assets.

There seem to be three main elements in the issue: alleged subservience to Britain; federal-provincial antagonism and suggested dominance by Ottawa; and an over-concentration on the symbolism of the Crown at the expense of an appreciation of its practical role in all governments of Canada, including that of Quebec.

It is not surprising that identification of the Crown with Brit-

---

*Until the late 1960's disagreements between French and English citizens in Quebec, disputes over federal-provincial relations, even issues over conscription, did not affect the position of the Crown in Quebec or the respect with which it was held in that province. The premiers were warm hosts to visiting royalty, and the public response was always enthusiastic. Even Mayor Camillien Houde of Montreal, who used to quip that he was the King's guest for four years in a concentration camp (put there by the Canadian government for impeding the war effort in the Second World War), entertained the King in Montreal, and was among the most memorable and cordial of all the King's hosts in Canada. Indeed Quebec City was the landing place for most visiting royalty and newly appointed Governors General, and the public welcomes there were spectacular introductions to Canada.

ain was fostered and criticized in the early 1960's when anti-British sentiments became fashionable in some intellectual and political circles at a time of declining British fortunes. Many of the critics then rushed to be counted as pro-American, even to identify with the U.S. presidency. By the early 1970's, however, to be anti-American became stylish with diminishing U.S. popularity in world affairs, along with growing participation by Americans, at Canada's invitation, in Canada's economic, educational, and cultural life, and with the effects of Watergate on the presidency. Much emotion accompanied these changes, and, as changing emotion always does, it left over-sensitivity and confusion in, among other things, attitudes toward the headship of state.

In Quebec, identification of the Crown with Britain was stated in a positive way in the words of Sir George E. Cartier already quoted: "If they had their institutions, their language and their religion intact today," he said of French-speaking Canadians, "it was precisely because of their adherence to the British Crown."[1] A century later a negative identification was illustrated by Dr. Marcel Chaput, the separatist leader: "For two hundred years," he declared, "the French-Canadians have been trying to free themselves from the British Crown, the symbol of foreign domination. . .French-Canadians have *never* accepted subjection to British Royalty. They simply endured it. . .the British Crown can mean only one thing: the free, voluntary and intentional acceptance of a tie."[2]

I have attempted to show in previous chapters that dominance by Britain was not a factor in the development of the Crown in Canada. All the evidence is the other way. Britain, like France before her, considered the northern colonies possessions of uncertain benefit with doubtful prospects, as indeed they were. They were not developed. They cost a great deal of money, and as they grew they looked to Britain to pay most of their bills, and to back and sell their bond issues at a time when they had no international standing whatever. Far from insisting on dependency and subservience, Britain encouraged them to stand on their own feet after responsible government, which they had trouble with; and during the discussions on union, which Britain encouraged but with which she did not interfere, even after Confederation when Canada needed all the help and money she could get to keep going and to establish her credentials as a nation. What, Dr. Chaput should explain, was the alternative? bankruptcy?

157

union with the United States? Furthermore, French Canadians were not the only ones not to have "accepted subjection" to Britain. All the colonists rejected it, as any colonists eventually do with a mother country. Actually, rejection of domination is the wrong concept; striking out on their own was what happened, and it took place as the colonists were able to do it. Neither French-speaking nor English-speaking Canadians have ever had to "endure" any degree of foreign domination not needed at the beginning and not invited later on. And, in comparison with other peoples, we do not know what it is. That we imagine and romanticize it sometimes, perhaps in words like those Dr. Chaput uses, involves little more than our tendency to forget that the provinces were once very young colonies.

Dr. Chaput mentioned "the free, voluntary and intentional acceptance of a tie" as if there was something wrong or degrading about it. We have discussed the practical aspects of the relationship in which the Crown is shared by countries in the Commonwealth. There is nothing degrading about it, because it now involves mutual benefit and friendship among independent and autonomous states at a time when the world desperately needs such relationships. That the tie does not now bind makes it the more blest. To identify the Crown as the British Crown may have been correct and practical years ago when Canada's own support of her institutions and foreign relations was not strong enough. But times have changed, and the Crown now belongs to Canada and other members of the Commonwealth separately, just as the name Chaput belongs separately and by right to all the family without any subservience implied by one to another.

This is all very well, a separatist might reply, but the French Canadian perceives the Crown as a foreign symbol and prefers Canadian or Quebec symbols. The problem here is not that the Crown is a foreign symbol, but that it is a shared symbol which we have made our own for practical reasons, and have either not recognized the fact or allowed doctrinaires to obscure it. Those who identify the Crown as foreign can as logically do the same thing with tartans, fleurs de lis, shamrocks, and almost every other symbol in Canada. And they can do it with parliament, the term "national assembly", the cabinet, the common law and the civil law in Quebec, even democracy itself, all of which we adopted from outside. Ukrainians, Jews, Asians, and others are still bringing in symbols and practices; and young people in Quebec and elsewhere are among the first to use them. Extreme leftists have adopted foreign doctrines and symbols, and even control from abroad, and yet have been active in Quebec. There is no danger in adopting symbols for local use in Quebec or any other province when there is no foreign dominance attached to their use. The dominance has long since gone from the Crown.

But does not national self-determination require purely local symbols, in this instance a Quebec presidency, for example? In adopting some kind of presidency Quebec would accept a foreign practice all over again, and still have to do what she has already done with the Crown–adapt it to Quebec. It is taking a long time for many countries to make presidencies adapt to their cultures. It would take longer in Quebec, which has been monarchal throughout its entire history. More fundamental, however, is the fact that nationalism of a kind that is based largely on symbolism and motivated by anti-something has generally failed every-where in the long run. Political units, institutions, language, even nationalism itself, are effective, strong and believable, not just when they have special status, but when they represent achieve-ment and quality of life. Even culture is effective only as it serves the people and not their politics disguised as nationalism. I reject any suggestion that Quebec lacks identity, achievement, quality of life, or culture to any greater extent than other provinces be-cause of Confederation. I fear that nationalism based on political emotionalism and localism may harm all four, without benefit to Quebec or anyone else, as it has in Ireland, Scotland, India, the Middle East, Africa, and other areas. On the other hand, the kind of nationalism that is based on political and cultural reali-ties, local achievements, and friendship with others is a splendid source of strength. For Quebec this kind of nationalism is not weakened, but fortified and enlarged, by the Crown.

The reasons I have given already. Every constitutional fact and political reality described in this book applies in full measure to Quebec, allows Quebec to be governed in Quebec's ways, and permits Quebec's public life to include adjustments and compen-sations for the vagaries of political fortune and the peculiarities of politicians and citizens. To say that Quebec is not a province like the others is true in some respects. But it is not true in the occur-rence of unusual political phenomena, the operation of political institutions, and the administration of political leaders–none of these is in any way peculiar to Quebec, or can be left to chance because of special Quebec circumstances.

I therefore include Quebec in all descriptions of the practical reasons for having the Crown in democratic government. It works in Quebec just as it works in the other provinces and in the federal government. But it works quietly and unostentatiously, as indeed it should, and for this reason its effectiveness can go unappreciated. "Je suis contre la monarchie," one eminent authority, Jean-Charles Bonenfant, told the Quebec National Assembly, "non pas par sentiment antibritannique, mais parce que je pense que c'est un système qui est aujourd'hui désuet."[3] He recommended an elected president.[4] As other pages indicate, the Crown is not out-of-date but modern, not purely ceremonial but practical, while presidencies vary in kind and stability and are often undemocractic. Practical questions must be asked. What alternatives to the Crown's functions, for example, would be used if Mr. Taschereau, Mr. Duplessis, and Mr. Barrette had been presidents instead of premiers? or if another kind of president were elected with their sponsorship? What is the answer to Mayor Drapeau's statement that "the French-Canadian people are royalists. What they want is a king."?[5] Or to the same sentiment expressed to Mr. Bonenfant in the Assembly by Mr. Lévesque (Laurier): "Les Canadiens français ne sont pas censés être royalistes"?[6] And what would happen if a president or prime minister could take advantage of this feeling and become in fact more monarchal than the Queen, and more gubernatorial than the Governor General or Lieutenant-Governor of Quebec, a situation that has occurred in many places with obvious results? To repeat an earlier comment, Quebec may be governed in a monarchy, but she is not governed monarchally.*

Criticism of the Crown based on federal-provincial antagonisms and alleged dominance by Ottawa is a tempting tactic to use, but an unfair one. There are bound to be antagonisms in a federal state. Of course Ottawa dominates; but so do the provinces, including Quebec, whenever they get the chance. This strain is characteristic of federalism, which system, by the way, John A. Macdonald only agreed to accept because Quebec (and the Maritimes) wanted it. But the Crown is not the symbol of the strain, although some critics have interpreted it this way; it was designed to relieve the strain. And Quebec was one of the first to

---

*The closest Quebec, or any province, has come to monarchy, indeed kingship in its purest form, was probably during the administration of Mr. Maurice Duplessis. How he ran his government personally is, for Canada, an incredible story.[7]

use it for this purpose. To illustrate, we must refer to an earlier discussion about the Crown's role in provincial government.

We have noted how the provinces received responsible government and Canada national independence at a minimum cost, and how the Crown permitted, indeed encouraged, the change. The same process operated within Canada. Quebec and all the other provinces retained identities, rights, cultures, and customs as Canada grew, not because the central government permitted them to do it, not because the provincial governments were always assiduous in preserving them, which they often were not, but because they enjoyed identities and rights guaranteed by the Crown and reinforced by its traditions. As a symbol it remained through the years while other temporary or would-be symbols emerged, flourished for awhile, and died. As a facilitator of political practice and compensator for human behaviour it helped government work at both national and local levels, without the ruthless control and standardization at either level which often crushes local ideas and practice elsewhere. Individual provinces benefited in particular ways, despite disadvantages such as the distance from the centre of British Columbia, the size of Prince Edward Island, the comparative poverty of Newfoundland, the shock of depression in the Prairies, the large size of Ontario, and the cultural differences in Quebec. None is a self-made province; all benefited from the system.

We have already noted that the provinces, including Quebec, were pretty flimsy communities at Confederation with little political experience and no economic affluence. The Crown gave all of them identity and status, indeed more than they could justify in a period when responsible government was not working well and it was likely they would be taken over by the United States unless they did something to prevent it. Contrary to some opinion, the provinces were not viable entities and strong cultures coming together for mutual benefit. Nevertheless, political leaders had to combine local pride with the exigencies of the moment and do something. Who took the lead? Quebec and Ontario, then known as the province of Canada.

Quebec critics often forget this basic fact of Confederation—that it was Quebec and only one other province, Ontario, that promoted union and that coaxed and convinced the others to join. Every one of the others joined only after dispute and misgiving during which Quebec was an active purveyor of the idea. Quebec critics may lament some of the results of

Confederation, but there are few current problems in the Maritimes and the West that were not foreseen in some form at the time of union and that were not the basis of assurances given by Quebec (and Ontario) to assuage doubts about the benefits of the great project. And these benefits have appeared in full measure to justify the predictions of the Fathers.

It should not be surprising, therefore, if eastern and western provinces said to Quebec (and Ontario): "You were the ones who proposed this union and who got us into it. You have done well out of it, and (don't quote us at the next federal-provincial conference) so have we. We have trouble dividing the spoils, but we must rejoice that there are ample spoils to divide. Some of us occasionally do better than others; but haves can become have-nots and vice versa. Confederation is not, therefore, a matter of continuing comfortable contentment in a changing world which is neither comfortable nor content. It is exactly what you (and Ontario) told us it would be when you invited us to join you." In the words of *Le Canadien* of Quebec, it was "the most acceptable solution for our future that politicians have yet been able to devise."[8]

"Furthermore," the other provinces could add, "we did not know you and you did not know us. We saw no pressing reasons for joining you. But there were two things we did have in common with you that helped bring us together and that *you* used to convince us—the British connection and the Crown. All of us saw the latter as a useful constitutional umbrella under which we could develop a federal partnership while maintaining our separate provincial systems. Your use of persuasion went pretty far. For example, you coaxed the Maritimes away from their own proposed union, and, although their trade had been with overseas ports and not with you, you convinced them to trade with you and come under the protective tariff which helped your industry. 'God Save the Queen' after all those banquets you gave us helped us to regard you as friends and to put our trust in the union; and it seemed preferable to the obvious alternative, 'O Say Can You See'."

If the Crown was a basis on which agreement could be reached in 1867, it was also a facilitator of discussions about the effects of union on Quebec a century later. The Crown permits the widest possible discussion of questions like "What does Quebec want?" and of the answers provided in reply. We may take this dialogue for granted. Nevertheless, there is a problem, ap-

162

parent in many other countries, of providing for the expression of demands and replies without governmental and factional assaults on free speech; allowing the will of the people, as distinct from that of debaters, to express itself in the clamour of debate; and permitting public business and citizens' lives to be carried on beneficially while the issues are discussed.

It is for these very reasons that what Quebec wants should include the Crown. No other constitutional arrangement permits such discussions so freely without violation of the rights, and disruption of the lives, of many citizens; without breakdown in governmental institutions; and without irreparable alienation of neighbours. It is easy to talk of political aspirations and raise intense emotions, but contemporary world affairs surely indicate that the aspirations fade in significance when the costs in blood, money, effective government, and citizens' happiness prove too high. Consequently many states subdue aspirations and emotions through autocratic presidential rule or military or party dominance. South America and Africa present many examples. So does Russia. "Separatist activity and preaching of national discord and chauvinism are deeply resented by Soviet people," said a document made available by the Soviet Embassy to the head of a Canadian news service. "In accordance with the people's will the Soviet law punishes with utmost severity any seditious conspiracy and activity. . .oriented to stir ethnic hatred."[9] The attitude is different in Canada, and it can be considered, not just on the basis of tolerating or persecuting critics, but on examining problems while doing two essential things—questioning the system and questioning the critics who may or may not represent either suitable alternatives or the will of the people. "We live in a place," said Premier Bourassa, "where freedom of expression and action is one of the greatest of all the countries of the world. Even the political parties who question the political system itself have every liberty to express themselves. Moreover, in the last few years, people have not failed to use this freedom of expression to spread hatred and lies systematically."[10] Because the headship of state in Quebec is a constitutional umbrella which both shelters opposition and guarantees the rights of all citizens as matters of principle and practice, the political ferment in Quebec has been more effective, and less dangerous for citizens, than similar contemporary demands for social and constitutional change under presidencies in other parts of the world.

To criticize the "federal presence" in Quebec is to undermine

163

the dual identity of citizens—federal and provincial—which all federalists regard as valuable. It is also to ignore the fact that the federal parliament and cabinet include many representatives of Quebec who participate in the "federal presence" in other provinces. As for the Lieutenant-Governor of Quebec, to say he represents dominance from Ottawa is to blame an official who has not dominated at all and whose presence has been overwhelmingly provincial. As we have noted, it is his connection with the Crown that has identified him as head of the province, that represents provincial autonomy, and that permits the provincial government to be as strong as it is while being responsible. Some Quebec observers have criticized the selection of the Lieutenant-Governor by the federal government, but, for reasons given earlier, there is no guarantee that selection by the provincial government would not destroy the powers of the office altogether.

This last possibility is readily forgotten by those who emphasize the power of the Quebec government as the custodian of Quebec's destinies. Who and what, it must be asked, will protect Quebec and its people from its own government? The same question can be asked in every province, just as it is now being asked in many countries.

There are now two forms of protection, and they *do* protect despite efforts to label them interference. One is the Crown, for reasons we have considered. The other is federalism, which, while it enables provincial governments to do much, provides another government to permit services and outlooks of a broader nature. The two may clash from time to time, but they do compensate for each other's weaknesses. Government leaders may chafe at limits on their authority. Doctrinaires who claim local autonomy as an inalienable right sound a seductive trumpet without stating what the nature of that autonomy may be, without indicating that separatism would involve a unitary system in Quebec, and without knowing what unforeseen circumstances may arise. The problems of local political autonomy, already described, can be noted in all provinces. Unforeseen and most undesirable circumstances can be illustrated by the bureaucratization and balkanization of higher education which followed the transfer of federal funds for universities to the provincial governments.*

---

*Provincial governments, ignoring the fact that half the money was federal, favoured local students in admission procedures and the provision of financial aid. Eventually students were encouraged to attend univer-

Far from being harmful, the federal presence has been healthy in all the provinces, just as the powerful provincial presence has been healthy in Ottawa. Whatever politicians and doctrinaires may say, the citizen is not served, and his rights are not preserved and increased, by either localism or centralization alone. And it is not only Quebec citizens that should guard their interests against excesses of either. Emphasized localism and over-dependence on the federal government are grave weaknesses in the Maritimes. That together each compensates for the other is the main reason why those provinces survive.

This view is contrary to that of Mr. Réné Lévesque, who dismisses the Canadian system with emotional force. "For the constitutional crisis has emphasized at least one thing on which there should be general agreement," he declared, "our present federal system is one of the most obsolete in the whole civilized world. It is an outdated, creaky, inefficient remnant of a 19th century colonial experiment in nation-building."[11]

World politics do not substantiate this assessment. In the first place, Mr. Lévesque himself illustrates the amount of democracy and freedom in Canada. He travels from coast to coast saying pretty much what he wants while being heard, liked for his charm, and respected for his ability, even while being questioned because of his intense, volatile emotion. He should tally the nations in which his counterparts could speak so freely and be accepted so cordially; there are very few. He should also consider what his rights to speak would be in a unitary Quebec if a future Maurice Duplessis treated him as the original Duplessis did Roncarelli.* In the second place, as we have noted, the Canadian system is modern because its institutions have changed with the times, even to the point where old forms have new meaning and ancient practices have modern results. Meanwhile throughout Mr. Lévesque's "whole civilized world," numerous states have adopted obsolete systems in trendy guise, including absolute

---

sities in their own province. Earlier, students from all parts of Canada got to know and understand one another while mixing at universities. Now local students meet too many of their own group and not enough from other places.

*Roncarelli was the plaintiff in an action brought against Mr. Duplessis in court when he lost his liquor license following the use of the Padlock Law against Jehovah's Witnesses in Quebec.

monarchs masquerading as presidents, family compacts and chateau cliques with the appearance of parties, and the military functioning as politicians. Mr. Lévesque should count the large number of constitutions and regimes that fell in the last sixty years, even in the last decade. And he might also assess the cost in lives, loss of freedom, and waste of resources involved in these changes. In the third place, judgements on political efficiency must give top priority to both the stability of states and their units and the kind of lives that ordinary citizens lead.

In all these respects, and by any comparisons, Canada, including Quebec, fares well. Of course her system is creaky. All systems tend to be, because the human beings who run them and propagate their political ideas are neither wholly manageable nor accurately predictable. Indeed it is desirable that her system be a bit creaky because it indicates some flexibility. Rigid, soundless systems are the ones to fear. They crack under stress and their citizens are too restricted. As for vintage, which is better for Canada, and Quebec—a nineteenth-century system that has changed with experience and that works, or a twentieth-century one that, like so many others of its time, is a revival of a long-discredited oligarchy, and has either not lasted or has given its people bad government, perhaps even insecure, unhappy lives?

I believe Mr. Lévesque's comment and others like it reflect a common misinterpretation of public business among politicians and doctrinaire critics of politics. The former, if they are not given many reminders, will tend to think in terms of their power when assessing ways of doing the public's business. The latter, if they are not watched and argued with, will interpret the public good in terms of the fulfillment of their special doctrines. Both readily invoke "rights" to back their claims. Yet the relevance of these "rights" may be of little or no real significance to the people in whose name they are proclaimed. For example, language rights, social services, cultural recognitions are real rights of people, especially if they are promoted as rights and not used as mere political tactics. But whose rights are increased or guaranteed when a university gets federal money from a provincial department? or when Mrs. Archambault gets a family allowance cheque signed by a provincial rather than a federal minister? One suspects that many issues are really game-playing with governmental procedures, which is inevitable, but which is really irrelevant, perhaps dangerous, if elevated to the status of a struggle for rights of no particular consequence to the people's welfare.

Many issues in Quebec, therefore, are not real issues at all, but the results of efforts of politicians, government departments, and doctrinaires, in the social services especially, to get political credits for doing favours and redistributing the people's money. And Quebec is not unique. Eastern provinces have long dressed up mere governmental wants as "Maritime rights", and imposed them along with real claims. And western governments have followed the example.

We might well improve federal-provincial relations if we made sharper, franker distinctions between what the governments and doctrinaires want and what the people want. Just as wars are started between governments and propagandists with little initial antagonisms between peoples, so are many quarrels between local units really based on administrative and ideological rivalry. The remedy, or at least the palliative, might well be some de-politicization in federal-provincial and inter-provincial relations.

A general view of over-politicization is not encouraging. Many antagonisms in and between nations are the consequences of too much concentration on political phenomena and political communication. Man has other interests, and these are much neglected in our concentration on government, the mechanics of securing political power, the personalities of political leaders, the propagation of political doctrines, and the purely political responsibilities of citizens. Indeed these interests may be violated altogether if the welfare of the state is confused with the interests of the government, especially if "the people" and "the government" are used synonymously. People rarely understand other people's politics, and if all they see is other people's politics, they rarely understand other people. Countless citizens do not understand their own politics, and if they are over-politicized they do not understand their own country and its place in the world. Politics are obviously important to public affairs, but if they are over-emphasized other activities in a society are eroded or distorted, particularly the most important ones of all—the cultural ones. Furthermore, politics is a unifying force in a state or province until it gets to the point where people take it too seriously and it becomes a divisive force splitting a people into unnecessarily antagonistic factions bolstered and embittered by hard-line stands.

Canada is no exception. Her unity will not thrive on politics alone, or on culture based on politics—the weakest of all forms of culture. Her relations with other nations will not thrive on political contacts alone. She is doomed to disappointment if she relies chiefly on political action to unite her people or establish her reputation abroad. The same is true within every province. Federal-provincial and interprovincial relations are essential, but there is much more to national and local understanding and goodwill than that. It is therefore time for non-political citizens and actions to be featured in relations among Canadians. Robert Bourassa and Réné Lévesque as politicians cannot exemplify, and should not be encouraged to exemplify, Quebec to Nova Scotians and British Columbians, but Gratien Gélinas and Monique Leyrac as artists can and do. In return T.C. Haliburton and Emily Carr can touch Quebec hearts quicker than any politicians. Tours by Bonhomme Carnaval in Alberta and Calgary's Young Canadians in Quebec speak clearly to people, and the Carnival and the Stampede are the pride of all Canadians. Direct contacts between citizens of Quebec and those of other provinces are more practical than the proxy contacts of politicians. One of the most successful projects in Canada's centennial year was the exchange tours of young people. To read the literature of the last decade on the crisis in Quebec one would think citizens of Quebec and of other provinces did not like each other. I suggest this assumption is not true. The antagonism is political, not cultural, and not personal. Citizens do not see and hear enough of one another directly. Even if everyone in Canada were bilingual, the situation would not change if people continue to communicate largely through the medium of politics. On the other hand, bilingualism would be hastened by cultural activity and personal contact, especially among young people. A Quebec poet emphasized the urgency of the matter. "J'ai été longtemps extrémement politisé," mused André Beauregard, "et je votais pour le parti québécois. Maintenant, je dis merde au parti québécois, merde à toute la politique. Si nous ne pensons qu'en terms politiques, nous sommes morts."[12]

One of the greatest assets of the Crown is its role as a much-needed de-politicizing instrument in government and in relations between government and the people. As we have noted, all politicians of all parties, civil servants, judges, and members of the armed services can relate to it because it is not in the possession, or under the influence, of any one group. Its representatives, named and advised by the people's representatives, are non-political in image because election has not forced them to be vote-getters to obtain their posts. All the practical, emergency, and decorative functions are designed to be non-political in character because they are best performed if they are. In Quebec, as in the other provinces, someone has to perform these functions, and the institutions of Queen, Governor General, and Lieutenant-Governor are designed specifically to do it. Certainly Quebec and the others must honour their premiers and ministers, but they will do it with greater safety if they salute their representatives of the Crown, keep its powers obvious but in reserve, and use its functions to represent government, not just politics, the community, and not just the political unit.

A sense of community, both provincial and national, is essential to federalism, indeed to any system. There is more to a state's government than the operation of constitutional machinery, more to its public philosophy than political doctrine, and more to its image than symbolism. A nation must seem to be a community to its people, and Canada is no exception. It requires elements that make up a community spirit: tradition, loyalty, respect, pride, emotion, and mysticism. Every state tries to encourage these elements in particular ways. Some are successful; many are not. The degree of success depends greatly on whether a state develops a mosaic or creates a striking pattern for its community spirit. The mosaic is varied, and is democratic in that it reflects passing phenomena, ideas, groups, and individuals, non-political as well as political, contemporary as well as traditional. There is something in it for everyone, and citizens can share it and concentrate on all of it, some of it, or none of it, as they wish. The striking pattern, on the other hand, tends to be temporary and relatively less democratic in most countries because it is associated too much with politics and with one era, group, or ideology. There is either too much or too little for citizens to concentrate on, which they must usually do whether they want to or not, because conforming to a political pattern tends to be compulsory.

Canada is a land of variety, and is so big that her sense of community requires constant attention. To encourage it the Crown features the mosaic, and its twelve representatives work in their jurisdictions to present the elements in it. Canadians all share the advantages, and can respond as they wish in any of the many ways available to them; and some may not want to respond at all at times and are not forced to do so. Because of the mosaic of human elements, administrations and policies, and public ideas and fashions can come and go with the shifting tides of public life, each making its own contribution, encouraged by a democratic variety, and unrestricted by a compulsory pattern. Meanwhile national feeling may rise and fall in intensity, but in the long run it grows because it is based on the continuity of changing traditions, rather than on an interrupted series of passing phenomena.

Maintaining a sense of community feeling is a major function of the Crown as the non-partisan location of executive power, and of the twelve people who represent it everywhere from Arachat to Malahat, from Parliament to Eskimo village. Other institutions also contribute to community feeling, and so do major works and citizens' achievements. The Crown recognizes as many of them as possible, something a politicized head of state rarely does, and symbolizes them all, both of which functions are designed to make the community feeling a national one, as well as a collection of local ones. "You have communicated to millions of Canadians," said Prime Minister Trudeau to Governor General Michener, "an enormous sense of exhilaration and enthusiasm—about your high office, about the Crown it represents and about the country we all love."[13] "The Governor General like the sovereign," Mr. Trudeau told Mr. Léger, "is the symbol of our unity as well as an agent of its preservation."[14]

Canadians do not always appreciate the result. Many of them have caught the powerful message of Canada's national spirit. They appreciate Canada's countless assets and compare what happens abroad with the experiences shared throughout Canada by their fellow citizens. Others tend to look for Utopias, ignore experiences elsewhere, emphasize weaknesses and neglect blessings, and wring hands over normal problems which they see as catastrophes. The first group sings O Canada! the second intones Oh! Canada. But the blessings are abundant, and the results are evident. A mere twenty-four million people are able to operate a peaceful nation in half a continent. All their governments have worked. And democracy has taken hold so well that political freedom is often unappreciated, even unrecognized. There are political problems, of course, but they are unavoidable in any system, and the wonder is that Canadians have had so few real ones.

To this situation the Crown and its twelve representatives are making a large and continuing contribution. They weave together the elements of national and community spirit through the institutions and processes of government, and provide compensations for human nature to help make democracy work.

.

NOTES

THE POLITICAL SETTING

1 See as an excellent study of democracy, R.M. McIver, *The Web of Government*, New York: Macmillan, 1947, pp. 175-244; and, by the same author, *The Modern State*, Oxford, 1955.

2 *Weekend Magazine*, July 12, 1975, p. 25.

3 British North America Act, s. 17.

4 Herbert Morrison, *Government and Parliament*, London: Oxford University Press, 1964, p. 106

5 Robert Menzies, *Afternoon Light*, London: Cassell, 1967,

p. 237.

6 Theodore H. White, *Breach of Faith: The Fall of Richard Nixon*, Toronto: McClelland and Stewart, 1975, p. 322.

7 Quoted in Robert Speaight, *Vanier*, Toronto: Collins, 1970, p. 431.

8 *The Guardian*, Charlottetown, July 19, 1975.

9 Confederation Debates, Canada, 1865, p. 33.

10 *Ibid*, pp. 59 and 62.

11 Donald Creighton, *Canada's First Century*, Toronto: Macmillan, 1970, p. 9.

THE HUMAN SETTING

1 Judy LaMarsh, *Memoirs of a Bird in a Gilded Cage*, Toronto: McClelland and Stewart, 1969, pp. 322-23, 343.

2 Hugh Trevor-Roper reviewing Nirad C. Chaudhuri's biography of Friedrich Max Muller, *Sunday Times*, London, Nov. 10, 1974. For a detailed discussion on this subject, with examples, see Frank MacKinnon, *Postures and Politics: Some Observations on Participatory Democracy*, Toronto: University

of Toronto Press, 1973, Chapters Five, Six, and Seven.

3 Hon. E.A. Forsey, *Senate Debates*, March 28, 1972, p. 268.

4 Mayor Mel Lastman of North York, *Canadian Magazine*, Oct. 6, 1973.

5 Calgary *Herald*, Feb. 14, 1974.

6 Calgary *Herald*, Nov. 30, 1975.

7 *The Times*, London, June 15, 1973.

8 Hon. J.P. Borowski, Minister of Transportation, Manitoba,

quoted in *Proceedings of the Special Joint Committee of the Senate and of the House of Commons on the Constitution of Canada*, 1972, session 2, issue 10.

9 Arthur M. Schlesinger, Jr., *The Imperial Presidency*, Toronto: Houghton Mifflin / Popular Library, 1974, p. 11.

THE ORGANIZATIONAL SETTING

1 Report, dated Sept. 3, 1973, of Queen Juliana's first interview with the press on Sept. 1, 1973. I am indebted to Canadian Ambassador Thomas Carter at The Hague for this report.

2 Durga Das, *India From Curzon to Nehru and After*, Calcutta: Rupa and Co., 1973, p. 365. This information was confirmed in a letter from Durga Das to the writer on June 14, 1973.

3 George Hutchinson in *The Times*, London, Jan. 4, 1975.

4 Robert Blake, *Unrepentant Tory*, New York: St. Martin's Press, 1956, p. 439.

5 James Stuart, *Within the Fringe*, London: The Bodley Head, 1967, p. 75.

6 Quoted by Governor General Vincent Massey, *Confederation on the March*, Toronto: Macmillan, 1965, p. 72.

7 *The Times*, London, July 1, 1971.

8 *Report from the Select Committee on the Civil List*, London: H.M.

Stationery Office, session 1972-72.

9 For the details of this cost see two articles by Philip Shaberoff of the New York *Times* in the *Globe and Mail*, Toronto, Jan. 3 and 4, 1974.

10 *The Times*, London, Sept. 17, 1973.

11 As far as Britain is concerned, an excellent account of the way the Queen's functions are handled and of the costs is contained in *Report from the Select Committee on the Civil List*, House of Commons, London; H.M. Stationery Office, session 1971-72. See also *The Times*, Feb. 12 and 13, and *Globe and Mail*, Toronto, Feb. 21, 1975.

12 Harold Nicolson, *King George V*, London: Pan Books 1967, p. 99; Herbert Morrison, *Government and Parliament*; London: Oxford, 1964, p. 97.

13 *The Economist*, Nov. 1973.

14 Robert Speaight, *Vanier*, p. 405.

THE QUEEN OF CANADA

1 L.B. Pearson, *Mike, the Memoirs of the Rt. Hon. L.B. Pearson*, Vol. II, Toronto: University of Toronto Press, 1973, pp. 106-07.

2 E.B. Greene, *The Provincial Governor*, New York, 1907, p. 9.

3 Dale C. Thomson, *Louis St. Laurent: Canadian*, Toronto:

Macmillan, 1967, p. 178.

4 *Final Report*, 1972, p. 29. A strong dissenting opinion by Senator Eugene Forsey, who was a member of the Committee, is in *Senate Debates*, March 23, 28, 29, 1972.

5 See report by the Associated Press on "Ebbing of World Press Freedoms", New York *Times*, Jan. 6, 1974.

6 The technical details of this change can be found in several sources. Three useful ones with

different approaches are: R. MacGregor Dawson, *The Government of Canada*, revised by Norman Ward, 5th ed., Toronto: University of Toronto Press, 1970, pp. 143-166; Ronald I. Cheffins, *The Constitutional Process in Canada*, Toronto: McGraw-Hill, 1969, pp. 93-110; and J.R. Mallory, *The Structure of Canadian Government*, Toronto, Macmillan, 1971, pp. 32-68.

7 *TV Times*, Jan. 11, 1974.

A TEAM OF GOVERNORS

1 *The Liquidators of the Maritime Bank of Canada vs. The Receiver General of New Brunswick*, (1892) A.C. 437.

2 Premier Robert Bourassa had published a book on James Bay during legal proceedings over a hydro-electric project, and refused at first to appear in court on contempt charges, although he did so later. Calgary *Herald* and other papers, Oct. 23, 1973.

3 Pierre Laporte, *The True Face of Duplessis*, Montreal: Harvest House, 1960, p. 50.

4 Toronto *Mail*, Nov. 6, 1873, quoted by Eugene A. Forsey in "Mr. King and Parliamentary Government", *The Canadian Journal of Economics and Political Science*, vol. XVII, no. 4, Nov. 1951, p. 464.

5 *Ibid.*

6 Robert Menzies, *Afternoon Light*, p. 258.

7 *Ibid*, p. 255.

8 For examples of alleged fed-

eral and provincial patronage see Peter C. Newman, *Renegade in Power*, Toronto: McClelland and Stewart, 1964, pages 285 and 372; and an editorial in *County Line Courier* (P.E.I.), October 30, 1974.

9 See John T. Saywell, *The Office of Lieutenant-Governor*, Toronto: University of Toronto Press, 1957; and the volumes on the provincial governments in the "Canadian Government Series" published by the University of Toronto Press.

10 Dale C. Thomson, *Louis St. Laurent: Canadian*, p. 324.

11 Robert L. Borden, "The Imperial Conference", *Journal of the Royal Institute of International Affairs*, July 1927, p. 204.

12 Vincent Massey, *What's Past is Prologue*, Toronto: Macmillan, 1963, p. 508.

13 H. Willis-O'Conner, *Inside Government House*, Toronto: The Ryerson Press, 1954, p.

70.

14 Vincent Massey, interviewed by Peter Newman, the Ottawa *Journal*, Feb. 25, 1967.

15 *Ibid.*

16 Vincent Massey, *What's Past is Prologue*, p. 509.

17 Speech at a banquet on Mr. Michener's retirement, described by Charles Lynch in the Calgary *Herald* and other papers, Jan. 9, 1974. Mr. Trudeau's exact words were: "I can testify that you are a man who knows, better than most, where the rocks ain't." Mr. Michener confirmed the relationship with satisfaction. "I was always," he said, "well advised and well treated and consulted by the government of the day." *The Albertan*, (Calgary) CP, Jan. 15, 1974.

18 Tony Cashman, *Vice-Regal Cowboy*, Edmonton: Institute of Applied Arts, 1957.

19 Herbert A. Bruce, *Varied Operations*, Toronto: Longmans, Green, 1958, pp. 223-33.

20 *Ibid.*

21 J.R. Smallwood in *The Gazette*, Montreal, July 8, 1972, p. 5. See also *I Chose Canada*, Toronto: Macmillan, 1973, p. 429.

22 Ernest Lapointe, House of Commons, *Debates*, 1932, p. 2,-989, quoted and discussed in John T. Saywell, *The Office of Lieutenant-Governor*, Toronto: University of Toronto Press, 1957, p. 264. Professor Saywell has included detailed discussion of various legal aspects and constitutional issues that concern the Lieutenant-Governor. Dr. Eugene Forsey and Professor J.R. Mallory have described constitutional aspects of both offices; the reader is referred to their articles in the bibliography. Issues in the provinces are also presented in the volumes on provincial government in "Canadian Government Series" published by the University of Toronto Press.

INFLUENCES ON EXECUTIVE POWERS

1 J.R. Mallory, "The Lieutenant-Governor's Discretionary Powers: The Reservation of Bill 56", *The Canadian Journal of Economics and Political Science*, vol. XXVII, no. 4, Nov. 1961, pp. 518-22.

2 Richard Gwyn, *Smallwood*, Toronto: McClelland and Stewart, 1972, pp. 210 and 221.

3 Judy LaMarsh, *Memoirs of a Bird in a Gilded Cage*, pp.

151-56.

4 R. MacGregor Dawson, *The Conscription Crisis of 1944*, Toronto, University of Toronto Press, 1961, p. 50.

5 This information resulted from interviews with parties involved. The premier was able to continue in office because the cabinet, while disagreeing with his action, disapproved of Johnston's advocacy of an ex-

tra judge. But the ministers learned that they should read minutes!

6 Calgary *Herald*, CP, Nov. 1, 1973.
7 Calgary *Herald*, March 29, 1975.
8 *The Sunday Times*, London, Aug. 5, 1973.
9 A.D.P. Heeney, "Some Aspects of Administrative Reform in the Public Service", *Canadian Public Administration*, vol. IX, no. 2, June, 1966, p. 223.

EMERGENCY POWERS

1 See Antonio Barrette, *Memoirs*, Montreal; Librairie Beauchemin, 1966, Chapters Eight, Thirteen, and Fourteen; and J.R. Mallory, "The Royal Prerogative in Canada: The Selection of Successors to Mr. Duplessis and Mr. Sauvé", *The Canadian Journal of Economics and Political Science*, vol. 26, no. 2, May, 1960, pp. 314-19.
2 Geoffrey Stevens, *Stanfield*, Toronto: McClelland and Stewart, 1973, p. 94.
3 *Ibid*, p. 66.
4 Lord Byng described his approach to the matter in a personal note published in Robert Speaight, *Vanier*, pp. 118-19; and in Byng to King George V, June 29, 1926, in Harold Nicolson, *King George V*, pp. 610-11.
5 Eugene Forsey, *The Royal Power of Dissolution of Parliament in the British Commonwealth*, Toronto; Oxford University Press, 1943.
6 M.S. Donnelly, *The Government of Manitoba*, Toronto; University of Toronto Press, 1963, pp. 118-19.
7 *TV Times*, Jan. 11, 1974.
8 R. MacGregor Dawson, *William Lyon Mackenzie King*, Toronto; University of Toronto Press, 1959, pp. 374-76.

DECORATIVE FUNCTIONS

1 Plutarch, *Lives*, New York: Collier, 1909, p. 48.
2 *The Times*, London, and other papers, Sept. 28. 1973.
3 See, for example, Charles Lynch on "redundancies, turgid titles and extravagant staffing" in the federal public service. Calgary *Herald* and other papers, Dec. 14, 1973.
4 Quoted in Frances FitzGerald, *Fire in the Lake*, Boston: Little, Brown, 1972, p. 445.
5 Bishop F.C. Kelly, *The Bishop Jots It Down*, New York, 1939, p. 29.
6 *The Star-Phoenix*, Saskatoon, Oct. 26, 1971.
7 Figures supplied through the courtesy of Mr. Esmond Butler, Secretary to the Governor General.

8 M.S. Donnelly, *The Government of Manitoba*, p. 119.
9 Calgary *Herald*, Dec. 14, 1973.

10 See *Public Accounts, Canada,* 1972-73, 8.4 and 8.5.

UNITY AND DIVERSITY

1 *Confederation Debates*, Canada, 1865, p. 62.
2 Marcel Chaput, *Why I Am A Separatist*, Toronto: The Ryerson Press, 1962, pp. 47-48.
3 *Débats de l'assemblée nationale du Québec*, le 14 aôut 1969, pp. 3021-55, spécialement p. 3,022.
4 *Ibid*, p. 2040.
5 *Time*, Nov. 11, 1974.
6 *Débats, op cit*, p. 3,037
7 See Pierre Laporte, *The True Face of Duplessis*.
8 *Le Canadien*, Quebec, Aug. 1, 1864, translation in P. B. Waite, *Confederation, 1854-1874,* Toronto: Holt, Rinehart and Winston, 1972, p. 98.
9 Charles Lynch, Calgary *Herald*, Nov. 23, 1974.

10 Quoted in Denis Smith, *Bleeding Hearts. . .Bleeding Country*, Edmonton: M.G. Hurtig, 1971, p. 83.
11 Réné Lévesque, "To Be Masters in Our Own House", in William Kilbourn, ed., *Canada, A Guide to the Peaceable Kingdom*, Toronto: Macmillan, 1970, p. 246.
12 Quoted in an article by Don Bell of Montreal in a Quebec supplement published by *Le Monde*, Paris, Dec. 1-2, 1974. The article was republished in English in *The Toronto Star*, Jan. 11, 1975.
13 The Calgary *Herald*, and other papers, Jan. 8, 1974.
14 *The Albertan*, Calgary, CP, Jan. 15, 1974.

SELECT BIBLIOGRAPHY

BOOKS

Anson, W.R. *The Law and Custom of the Constitution*. London, 1935.

Bagehot, Walter. *The English Constitution*. London, 1867.

Barrette, Antonio. *Memoirs*. Montreal, 1966.

Beck, J. Murray. *The Government of Nova Scotia*. Toronto, 1957.

Bruce, Herbert A. *Varied Operations*. Toronto, 1958.

Canada. *Confederation Debates*. 1865.

Canada. *Proceedings of the Special Joint Committee of the Senate and of the House of Commons on the Constitution of Canada*. 1972.

Cashman, Tony. *Vice-Regal Cowboy*. Edmonton, 1957.

Cheffins, R.I. *The Constitutional Process in Canada*. Toronto, 1969.

Corry, J.A. and J.E. Hodgetts. *Democratic Government and Politics*. Toronto, 1959.

Dawson, R. MacGregor, revised by Norman Ward. *The Government of Canada*. Toronto, 1970.

Dawson, R. MacGregor. *The Principle of Official Independence*. London, 1922.

Dicey, A.V. *Introduction to the Study of the Law of the Constitution*. London, 1961.

Donnelly, M.S. *The Government of Manitoba*. Toronto, 1963.

Forsey, Eugene A. *Freedom and Order*. Toronto, 1974.

_____ . *The Royal Power of Dissolution of Parliament in the British Commonwealth*. Toronto, 1943.

Graham, Roger. *The King-Byng Affair, 1926: A Question of Responsible Government*. Toronto, 1967.

Greene, E.B. *The Provincial Governor*. New York, 1907.

Gwyn, Richard. *Smallwood*. Toronto, 1972.

Hendry, J. McL. *Memorandum on the Office of Lieutenant-Governor of a Province*. Ottawa, Department of Justice, 1955.

Jennings, W. Ivor. *Cabinet Government*. London, 1959.

_____ . *The British Constitution*. London, 1966.

_____ . *The Law and the Constitution*. London, 1959.

Keith, A.B. *The Dominions as Sovereign States*. London, 1938.

———. *Responsible Government in the Dominions.* Oxford, 1928.

La Forest, G.V. *Disallowance and Reservation of Provincial Legislation.* Ottawa, 1955.

Laporte, Pierre. *The True Face of Duplessis.* Montreal, 1960.

MacIver, R.M. *The Modern State.* Oxford, 1955.

———. *The Web of Government.* New York, 1965.

MacKinnon, Frank. *The Government of Prince Edward Island.* Toronto, 1951.

———. *Postures and Politics.* Toronto, 1973.

Massey, Vincent. *What's Past is Prologue.* Toronto, 1963.

Mallory, J.R. *The Structure of Canadian Government.* Toronto, 1971.

Morrison, Herbert. *Government and Parliament.* London, 1964.

Nicolson, Harold. *King George V–His Life and Reign.* London, 1952.

O'Connor, H. Willis. *Inside Government House.* Toronto, 1954.

Saywell, John T. *The Office of Lieutenant-Governor.* Toronto, 1957.

Speaight, Robert. *Vanier.* Toronto, 1970.

H.M. Stationery Office. London. *Report from the Select Committee on the Civil List.* Session 1971-72.

Thorburn, Hugh G. *Politics in New Brunswick.* Toronto, 1961.

Ward, Norman and Duff Spafford, eds. *Politics in Saskatchewan.* Toronto, 1968.

ARTICLES

Dawson, R. MacG., "The Independence of the Lieutenant-Governor", *Dalhousie Review*, vol. II, July, 1922.

Forsey, E.A., "Mr. King and Parliamentary Government", *Canadian Journal of Economics and Political Science*, vol. XVII, no. 4, November, 1951.

———, "The Crown and the Constitution," *Dalhousie Review*, vol. XXXIII, Spring, 1953.

———, "Constitutional Monarchy and the Provinces", *The Confederation Challenge* (Ontario Advisory Committee on Confederation, Background Papers and Reports), vol. I, 1967.

———, "The Problem of 'Minority' Government in Canada", *Canadian Journal of Economics and Political Science*, vol. XXX, no. 1, February, 1964.

———, "Disallowance of Provincial Acts, Reservation of Provincial Bills, and Refusal of Assent by Lieutenant-Governors since 1867", *Canadian Journal of Economics and Political Science*, vol. IV, February, 1938.

———— , "Lieutenant-Governors are not Ambassadors", *Saturday Night*, March 20, 1948.

Franct, T., "The Governor General and the Head of State Functions", *Canadian Bar Review*, vol. 32, no. 10, December, 1954.

Kennedy, W.P.M., "The Office of Governor General of Canada", *Canadian Bar Review*, vol. 31, no. 9, November 1953.

MacKinnon, Frank, "The Crown in a Democracy," *Dalhousie Review*, vol. 49, no. 2, Summer 1969; *Commonwealth Journal*, vol. XII, no. 6, December 1969.

———— , "The Royal Assent in Prince Edward Island: Dissallowance of Provincial Acts, Reservations of Provincial Bills, and the Giving and Withholding of Assent by Lieutenant-Governors", *Canadian Journal of Economics and Political Science*, vol. XV, May 1949.

Mallory, J.R., "The Royal Prerogative in Canada: the Selection of Successors to Mr. Duplessis and Mr. Sauvé", *Canadian Journal of Economics and Political Science*, vol. XXVI, no. 2, May 1960.

———— , "The Appointment of the Governor General: Responsible Government, Autonomy, and the Royal Prerogative", *Canadian Journal of Economics and Political Science*, vol. XXVI, no. 1, February 1960.

———— , "The Lieutenant-Governor's Discretionary Powers: The Reservation of Bill 56," *Canadian Journal of Economics and Political Science*, vol. XXVII, no. 4, November 1961.

———— , "The Lieutenant-Governor as a Dominion Officer: The Reservation of the Three Alberta Bills in 1937", *Canadian Journal of Economics and Political Science*, vol. 14, no. 4, November 1948.

McWhinney, Edward, "Prerogative Powers of the Head of State," *Canadian Bar Review*, vol. XXXV, no. 1, January 1957, and E.A. Forsey and J.R. Mallory thereon, *ibid.*, nos. 2 and 3.

Morton, W.L., "Meaning of Monarchy in Confederation", Royal Society of Canada, *Transactions*, Fourth series, vol. 1, 1963.

Saywell, John T., "Reservation Revisited, Alberta, 1937," *Canadian Journal of Economics and Political Science*, vol. XXXVII, no. 3, August 1961.

181

INDEX

183

184

sovereign, see Crown
Spain, 27, 84
Speaight, Robert, 68n, 130n
Stalin, J., 46, 55
Stanfield, Robert, 126
state, definition of, 17
Stevens, Geoffrey, 126n
Stratford Festival, 137
Stuart, James, 59n
Sukarno, President, 84
Supreme Court, 115n
Switzerland, 85

Taiwan, 85
Taylor-Burton marriage, 139
Thompson, Sir John, 125
Thomson, Dale C., 76n, 101n
Tito, Marshal, 144
traditions, 72-4, 77-8, 82, 169-71
Trudeau, Pierre, 31, 34, 47
    and Governor General, 103, 170
trust, powers in, 17, 35, 72, 88
Tupper, Sir Charles, 132
Tweedsmuir, Lord, 95, 101

Uganda, 68-9
United States
    and Canadian federalism, 28, 30,
        156
    political puritanism in, 137
    president of, see president, U.S.
    lack of prime minister in, 86
unity, national, 154-71

Vanier, Georges, 68, 95, 103, 112,
    142, 156
Vanier, Mrs. Pauline, 100
veto power, 107-9
Victor Emmanuel, King, 45

Waite, Peter B., 162n
Ward, Norman, 88n
Watergate, 25, 46, 61, 127, 156
White, Theodore H., 25
Wilhelm II., Emperor, 48
Wilhelmina, Queen, 45
Wilson, Woodrow, 35
worshipping tendencies, 34-6, 116

Young Canadians, The, 168

189